T0046903

ENGLISH FOR EVERYONE JUNIOR

BEGINNER'S COURSE

PRACTICE BOOK

FREE AUDIO
website and app

www.dkefe.com/junior/us

Author

Ben Ffrancon Davies is a freelance writer and translator. He writes textbooks and study guides on a wide range of subjects including ELT, history, and literature. He also works on general nonfiction books for children and adults. Ben studied Medieval and Modern Languages at the University of Oxford, and has taught English in France and Spain.

Course consultant

Susannah Reed is an experienced author and educational consultant, specializing in Primary ELT materials. She has taught in Spain and the UK and has worked in educational publishing for over 20 years, as both a publisher and a writer of ELT course books for children around the world.

Language consultant

Professor Susan Barduhn is an English-language teacher, teacher trainer, and author, who has contributed to numerous publications. She has been President of the International Association of Teachers of English as a Foreign Language, and an adviser to the British Council and the US State Department. She is currently a professor at the School of International Training in Vermont.

ENGLISH FOR EVERYONE JUNIOR

BEGINNER'S COURSE

PRACTICE BOOK

FREE AUDIO
website and app

www.dkefe.com/junior/us

Penguin Random House

Senior Editor Ben Ffrancon Davies
Senior Art Editor Amy Child
Illustrators Amy Child, Dan Crisp
Managing Editor Carine Tracanelli
Managing Art Editor Anna Hall
Senior Production Editor Andy Hilliard
Production Editor Gillian Reid
Senior Production Controllers Samantha Cross, Jude Crozier
Jacket Design Development Manager Sophia MTT
Senior Jacket Designer Surabhi Wadhwa-Gandhi
Jacket Designer Juhi Sheth
Senior Jackets Coordinator Priyanka Sharma-Saddi
DTP Designer Rakesh Kumar
Publisher Andrew Macintyre
Associate Publishing Director Liz Wheeler
Art Director Karen Self
Publishing Director Jonathan Metcalf

First American Edition, 2022
Published in the United States by DK Publishing
1450 Broadway, Suite 801, New York, NY 10018

Copyright © 2022 Dorling Kindersley Limited
DK, a Division of Penguin Random House LLC
22 23 24 25 26 10 9 8 7 6 5 4 3 2 1
001–322065–Mar/2022

All rights reserved.
Without limiting the rights under the copyright reserved above, no part of this publication may be reproduced, stored in or introduced into a retrieval system, or transmitted, in any form, or by any means (electronic, mechanical, photocopying, recording, or otherwise), without the prior written permission of the copyright owner.
Published in Great Britain by Dorling Kindersley Limited

A catalog record for this book
is available from the Library of Congress.
ISBN 978-0-7440-2846-1

DK books are available at special discounts when purchased
in bulk for sales promotions, premiums, fund-raising, or educational use.
For details, contact: DK Publishing Special Markets,
1450 Broadway, Suite 801, New York, NY 10018
SpecialSales@dk.com

Printed and bound in China

For the curious

www.dk.com

MIX
Paper from responsible sources
FSC™ C018179
FSC
www.fsc.org

This book was made with Forest Stewardship Council ™ certified paper – one small step in DK's commitment to a sustainable future.
For more information go to
www.dk.com/our-green-pledge

Contents

About the course 6

1 My friends 10

2 At school 16

3 Our classroom 24

4 My things 30

5 Our favorite animals 38

6 This is my family 46

7 This is my room 54

8 Review: This is me 62

9 At the fair 64

10 Our pets 72

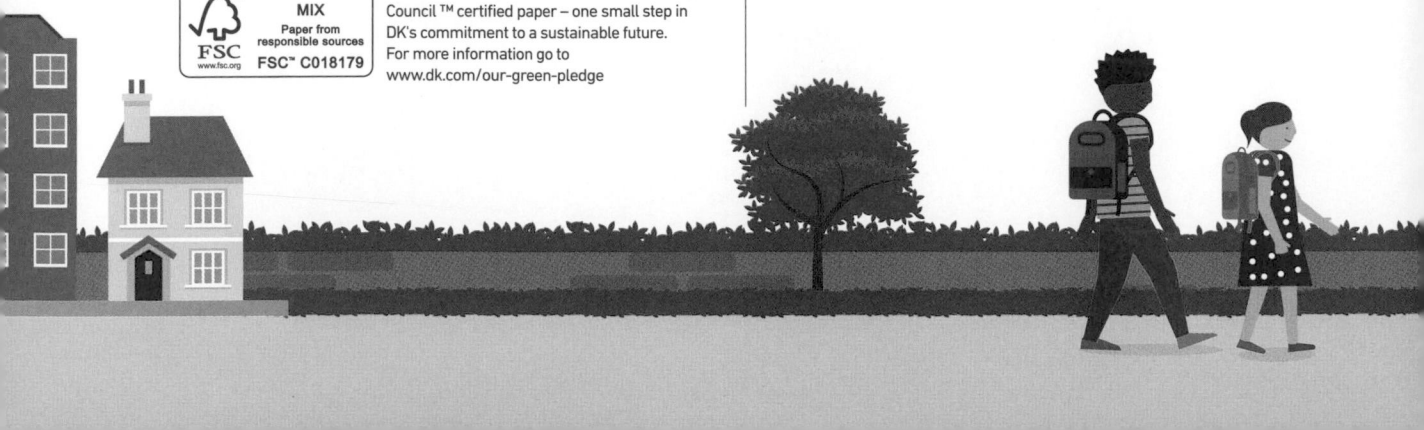

11 My body 80

12 Our town 88

13 My home 96

14 Review: Where I live 104

15 On the farm 106

16 Sports 114

17 At the food market 124

18 At the toy store 132

19 Our hobbies 140

20 Review: What I like 148

21 Our party clothes 150

22 Our day at the beach 158

23 Lunchtime 166

24 At the park 174

25 My day 182

26 Review: Me and my day 192

Handwriting guide 194

Answers 199

Acknowledgments 224

About the course

English for Everyone Junior: Beginner's Practice Book is a companion to the *English for Everyone Junior: Beginner's Course*. The course book is divided into 26 units—each with its own theme—and the practice book mirrors that structure. There is audio for all the units.

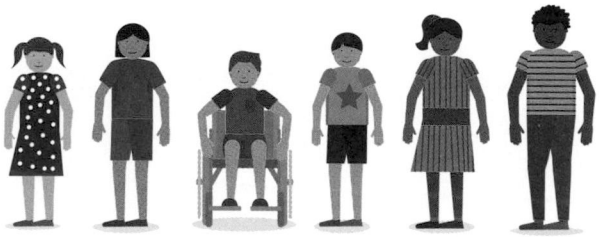

Our characters

A group of six friends—Maria, Sofia, Ben, Andy, Sara, and Max help you practice language in a natural and friendly way.

Unit structure

Each practice unit starts with a scene that presents the vocabulary taught in the corresponding course book unit. The child then practices this vocabulary along with the grammar rules they learned in that unit of the course book.

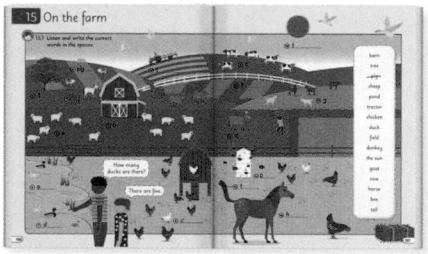

1 New vocabulary

The illustrated scene helps the child practice the vocabulary, as they listen to each word and write it in the correct space.

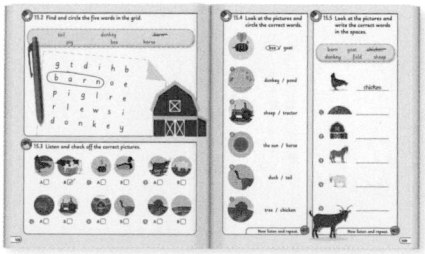

2 Vocabulary practice

There is more vocabulary practice. The child might be asked to match vocabulary to pictures or spell individual words.

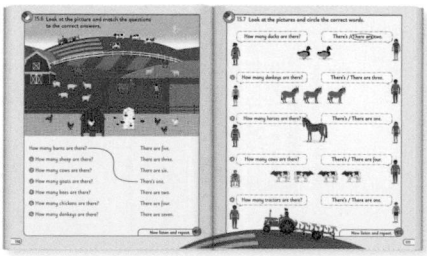

3 Grammar practice

Each unit then practices the grammar rules taught in the corresponding course book unit while also studying vocabulary.

4 Grammar practice

More grammar is practiced. Many units also have a song to help learn new grammar and vocabulary.

Audio

English for Everyone Junior: Beginner's Practice Book features extensive supporting audio resources. Listening to and repeating the audio recordings will help the child master the pronunciation and stress patterns of English, as well as help them to cement new language in their memory.

Register at **www.dkefe.com/junior/us** to access the audio materials for free. Each file can be played, paused, and repeated as often as you like.

All vocabulary scenes, songs, and listening exercises have accompanying audio.
Clicking on the corresponding number on the app will play the relevant audio file.

Most exercises have accompanying audio. After completing an exercise, the child should listen to the correct answers and then repeat them out loud.

FREE AUDIO
website and app

www.dkefe.com/junior/us

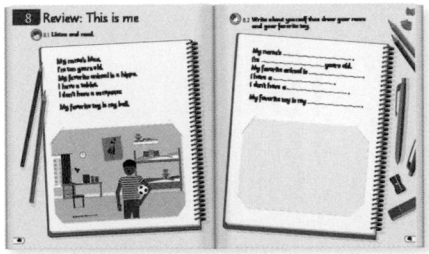

Review units

Four review units provide the child with a chance to read a text incorporating vocabulary and grammar from recent units. The child then writes a personalized answer based on this text.

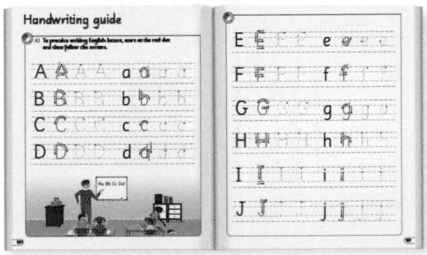

Handwriting guide

The book includes a guide explaining how to form each letter of the English alphabet. The child has space to practice the formation of each letter.

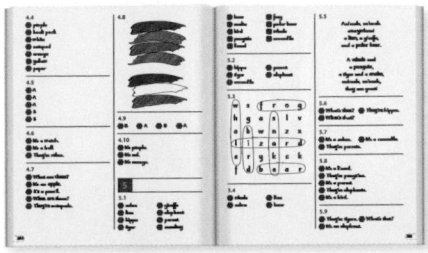

Answers

At the back of the book, answers to all the exercises are clearly presented. Key information is sometimes shown in bold to make it easier to grade the child's work.

Practicing new vocabulary

Each unit opens with an illustrated scene that matches the course book, but with the words removed and placed in a panel. The parent or teacher should supervise the child as they listen to the accompanying audio on the website or the app and write the correct words in the spaces.

1 First, click on the corresponding unit number (here, **Unit 15**) on your screen. Then, click on the exercise number and play each audio file in turn.

All the words needed to 2 complete the scene are given in a word pool.

3 After listening to each word, the child should write it down in the correct space, using the panel to help them.

4 After completing the scene by writing in all the words, press **Play all** to listen to all the words again.

5 The audio pauses for a few seconds after each word. The child should repeat the word during this pause.

Practicing new grammar

Grammar is practiced in the same order that it is taught in the corresponding course book unit. Throughout the grammar exercises, vocabulary from the unit is repeated and recycled to help the child memorize it and see it used in context.

1 After revising vocabulary, the child then practices the grammar from the corresponding course book unit in exercises that reuse the unit's vocabulary.

2 Use the exercise number (here, **15.9**) to find the answers for each exercise at the back of the book, starting on page 199.

15.8 Look at the pictures and write the correct words in the spaces.

behind ~~in~~ next to in front of

Where are the cows?
They're in the field.

1 Where's the horse?
It's _____ the tree.

2 Where's the donkey?
It's _____ the pond.

3 Where are the goats?
They're _____ the barn.

Now listen and repeat.

112

15.9 Listen to the song and write the correct words in the spaces.

Where are the ducks ?
They're in the _____ !

Where are the _____ ?
They're _____ the field!

Where are the _____ ?
They're in the _____ !

_____ are the animals?
They're _____ my farm!

15.10 Look at the pictures and check off the correct sentences.

The donkey's in the field. ☑
The donkeys are in the field. ☐

1 The duck's in the pond. ☐
The ducks are in the pond. ☐

2 The sheep's in front of the barn. ☐
The sheep are in front of the barn. ☐

3 The horse is under the tree. ☐
The horses are under the tree. ☐

Now listen and repeat.

113

3 Most exercises have an audio recording so the child can listen to the questions and correct answers after completing each exercise.

4 All the songs from the course book are repeated, but with some words removed. The child should listen to the song and write the correct words in the spaces.

1 My friends

1.1 Listen to the children and write their names in the spaces.
Hello, I'm Maria. What's your name?
Hi, I'm Max.
Hello, I'm Ben.
① Maria
② B
③ M

Ben ~~Maria~~ Andy
Sara Sofia Max
Hi, I'm Andy. What's your name?
Hi, my name's Sara.
Hello, my name's Sofia.
4 A
5 S
6 S

1.2 Listen and write the correct words in the spaces.

I'm Maria ~~Hello~~ Max Hello name's

Hello, my name's Sofia.

1 

Hi, my _____ Sara.

2 

Hi, I'm _____.

3 

Hi, _____ Andy.

4 

Hello, I'm _____.

5 

_____, I'm Ben.

1.3 Find Max and Sara in the picture.

1.4 Listen and circle the correct names.

Ben / Maria

1

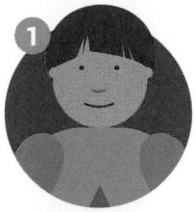

Andy / Sofia

2

Maria / Sara

3

Andy / Max

4

Maria / Sofia

5

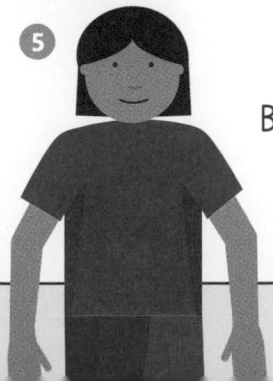

Ben / Sofia

1.5 Match the numbers to the correct words.

1 — seven

1 **3** — one

2 **7** — six

3 **9** — three

4 **6** — eight

5 **10** — five

6 **8** — nine

7 **5** — ten

Now listen and repeat.

1.6 Listen and color in the numbers you hear.

73 1 18 2 62

3 84 4 51 5 79

1.7 Count and write the correct numbers under the pictures.

t h r e e

1 ___ ___ ___

2 ___ ___ ___

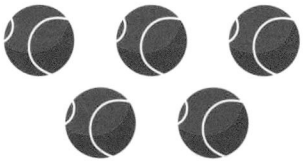

3 ___ ___ ___ ___

4 ___ ___ ___ ___

5 ___ ___ ___

Now listen and repeat.

1.8 Match the questions to the correct answers.

Hello, what's your name?

1 How are you?

2 How old are you?

I'm nine years old.

My name's Sara.

I'm fine, thanks.

Now listen and repeat.

I'm eight years old.
How old are you?

And you?

I'm _____
years old.

2 At school

2.1 Listen and write the correct words in the spaces.

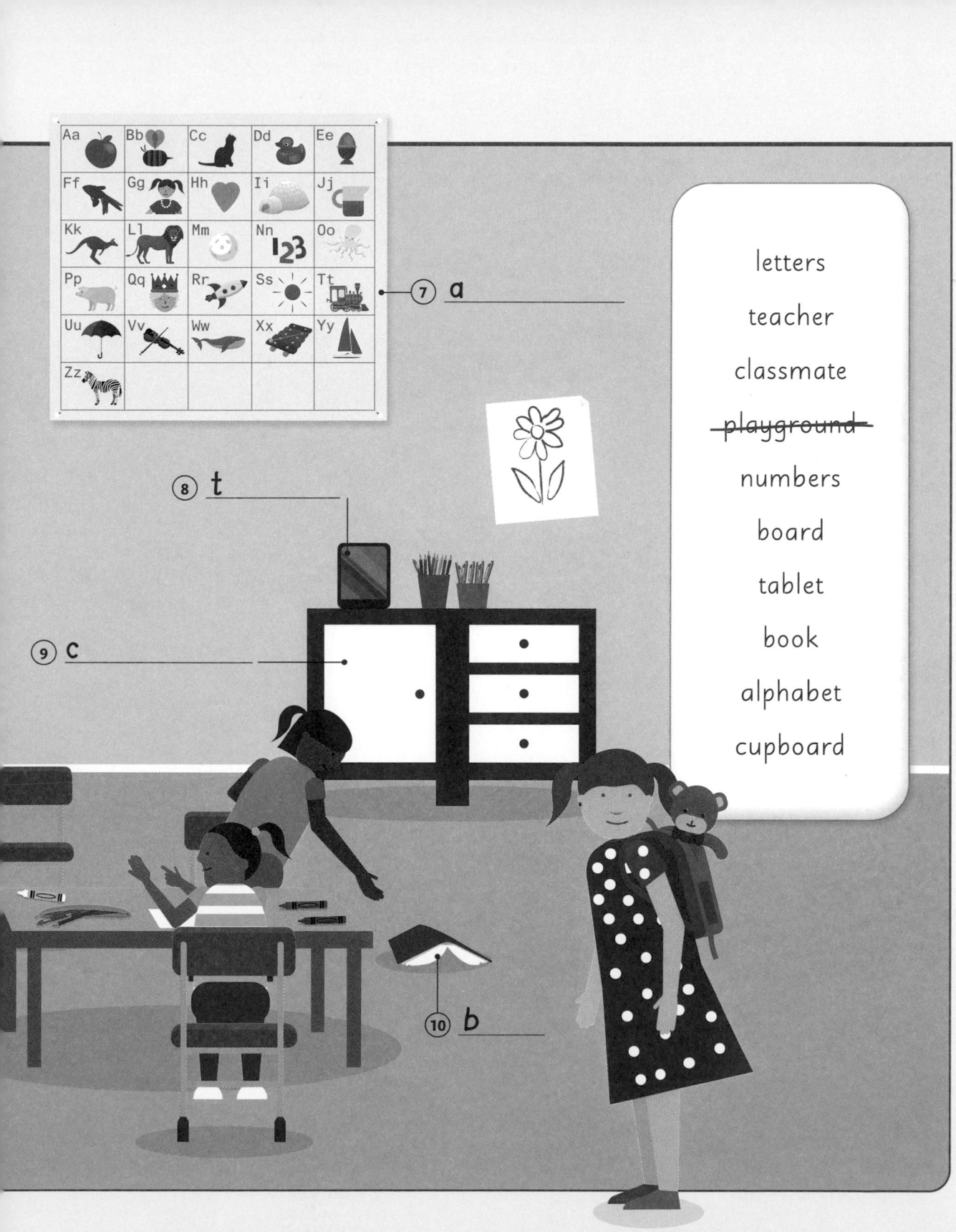
Aa Bb Cc Dd Ee
Ff Gg Hh Ii Jj
Kk Ll Mm Nn Oo
123
Pp Qq Rr Ss Tt
Uu Vv Ww Xx Yy
Zz
7 a
8 t
9 c
10 b
letters
teacher
classmate
~~playground~~
numbers
board
tablet
book
alphabet
cupboard

2.2 Look at the pictures and check off the correct words.

numbers ☐
book ☑

1

tablet ☐
board ☐

2

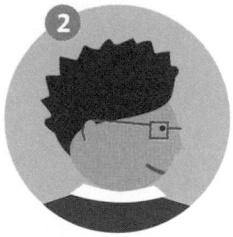

teacher ☐
letters ☐

3

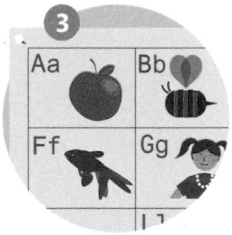

cupboard ☐
alphabet ☐

4

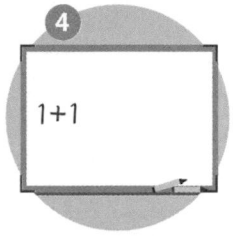

board ☐
classmate ☐

5

playground ☐
book ☐

6

numbers ☐
letters ☐

7

numbers ☐
cupboard ☐

8

board ☐
classmate ☐

9

tablet ☐
cupboard ☐

Now listen and repeat.

2.3 Look at the pictures and write the words in the correct place on the crossword.

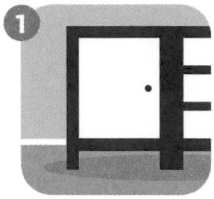

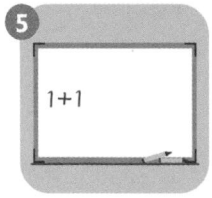

2.4 Listen and check off the correct pictures.

A ☐

B ☑

1 A ☐

B ☐

2 A ☐

B ☐

3 A ☐

B ☐

4 A ☐

B ☐

5 A ☐

B ☐

2.5 Match the pictures to the correct words.

find

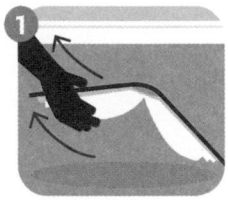

add

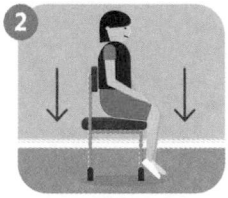

stand up

ask

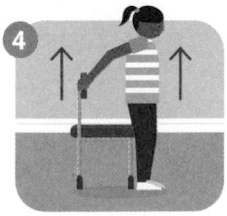

pick up

sit down

Now listen and repeat.

2.6 Look at the pictures and write the correct words in the spaces.

find close ~~open~~
answer show listen

open

_____

_____

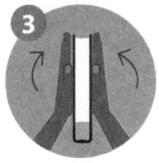

_____

_____

_____

Now listen and repeat.

2.7 Look at the pictures and write the letters in the correct order.

l s t i n e

l i s t e n

f d n i

1 f _ _ _

a k s

2 a _ _

s o w h

3 s _ _ _

l k o o

4 l _ _ _

o n p e

5 o _ _ _

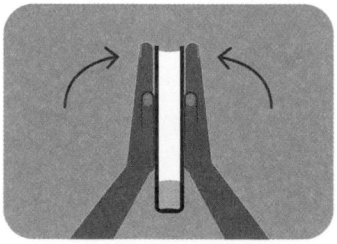

c s o l e

6 c _ _ _ _

d d a

7 a _ _

a r w e s n

8 a _ _ _ _ _

Now listen and repeat.

2.8 Look at the pictures and circle the correct words.

His / Her name's Sara.

1 His / Her name's Andy.

2 His / Her name's Ben.

3 His / Her name's Maria.

4 His / Her name's Max.

5 His / Her name's Sofia.

Now listen and repeat.

2.9 Listen and match the questions to the correct answers.

What's his name?	Her name's Bella.
1 What's his name?	His name's Tom.
2 What's her name?	Her name's Amy.
3 What's his name?	His name's Ted.
4 What's her name?	His name's Dan.
5 What's her name?	Her name's Anna.

2.10 There are four sentences. Mark the beginning and end of each one and write them below.

What's her name? _____

1 _____

2 _____

3 _____

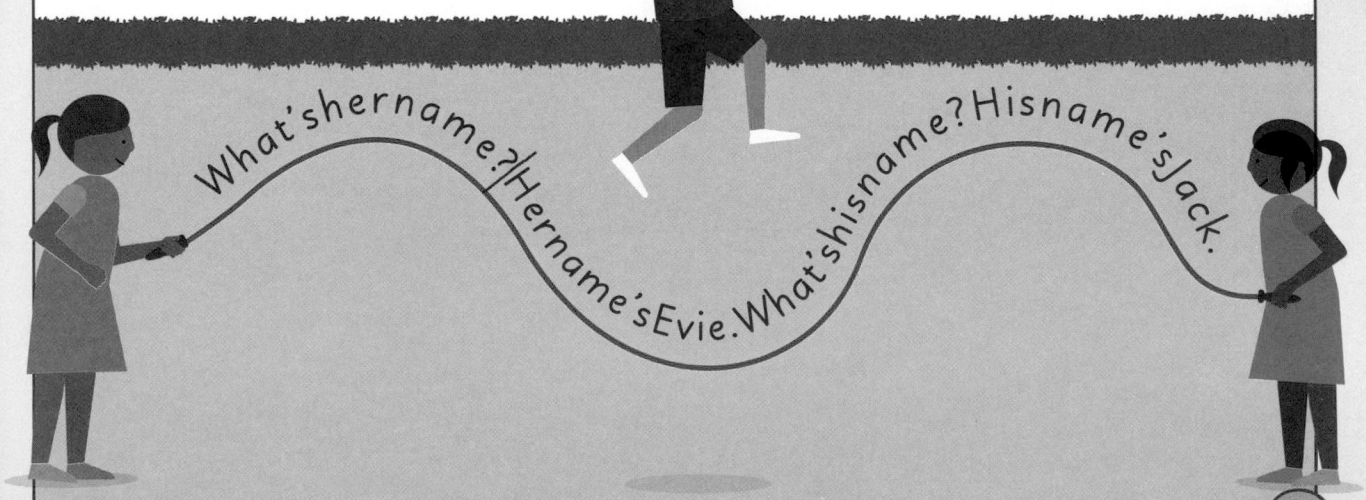

Now listen and repeat.

3 Our classroom

3.1 Listen and write the correct words in the spaces.

4 p
count
~~write~~
read
paint
play
draw
spell
5 s
A
B C
cat
Let's study English!
6 p
7 d

3.2 Look at the pictures and circle the correct words.

draw / count

read / play

play / spell

draw / write

paint / count

Now listen and repeat.

3.3 Listen and check off the correct pictures.

A ☐ B ☑

1 A ☐ B ☐

2 A ☐ B ☐

3 A ☐ B ☐

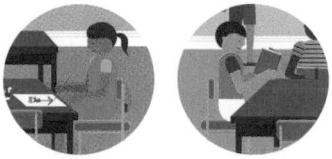

4 A ☐ B ☐

5 A ☐ B ☐

3.4 Match the pictures to the correct sentences.

Let's count!

Let's draw!

Let's read!

Let's write!

Let's play!

Let's paint!

Now listen and repeat.

3.5 Listen to the song and write the correct words in the spaces.

Hello, hello !
What's your _____ ?
How are you?
Let's _____ a game.

_____ say hello
to my new friends
_____ and Maria,
Sara and _____ .

3.6 Match the numbers to the correct words.

17 1 12 2 16 3 15 4 20

sixteen

seventeen

twenty

twelve

fifteen

Now listen and repeat.

3.7 Write the correct words under the numbers.

eighteen ~~twelve~~ eleven fourteen twenty thirteen nineteen sixteen fifteen

12 twelve

1 14 _____

2 19 _____

3 18 _____

4 11 _____

5 16 _____

6 20 _____

7 13 _____

8 15 _____

Now listen and repeat.

3.8 Look at the pictures and circle the correct words.

book / books

1 

tablet / tablets

2 123

number / numbers

3 

car / cars

4 

dog / dogs

5 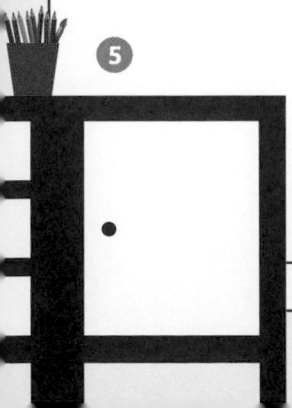

cupboard / cupboards

Now listen and repeat.

3.9 Read the words and check off the correct pictures.

pen

A ☐

B ☑

1 cat

A ☐

B ☐

2 letters

A ☐

B ☐

3 chair

A ☐

B ☐

4 dolls

A ☐

B ☐

Now listen and repeat.

4 My things

4.1 Listen and write the correct words in the spaces.

crayon	~~pink~~	
book	pen	eraser
ball	paper	notepad
book pack	purple	ruler
white	red	brown
green	apple	yellow
orange	pencil	blue
gray	watch	black

① pink

② b

③ c

④ e

⑤ p

⑥ p

⑦ b

⑧ n

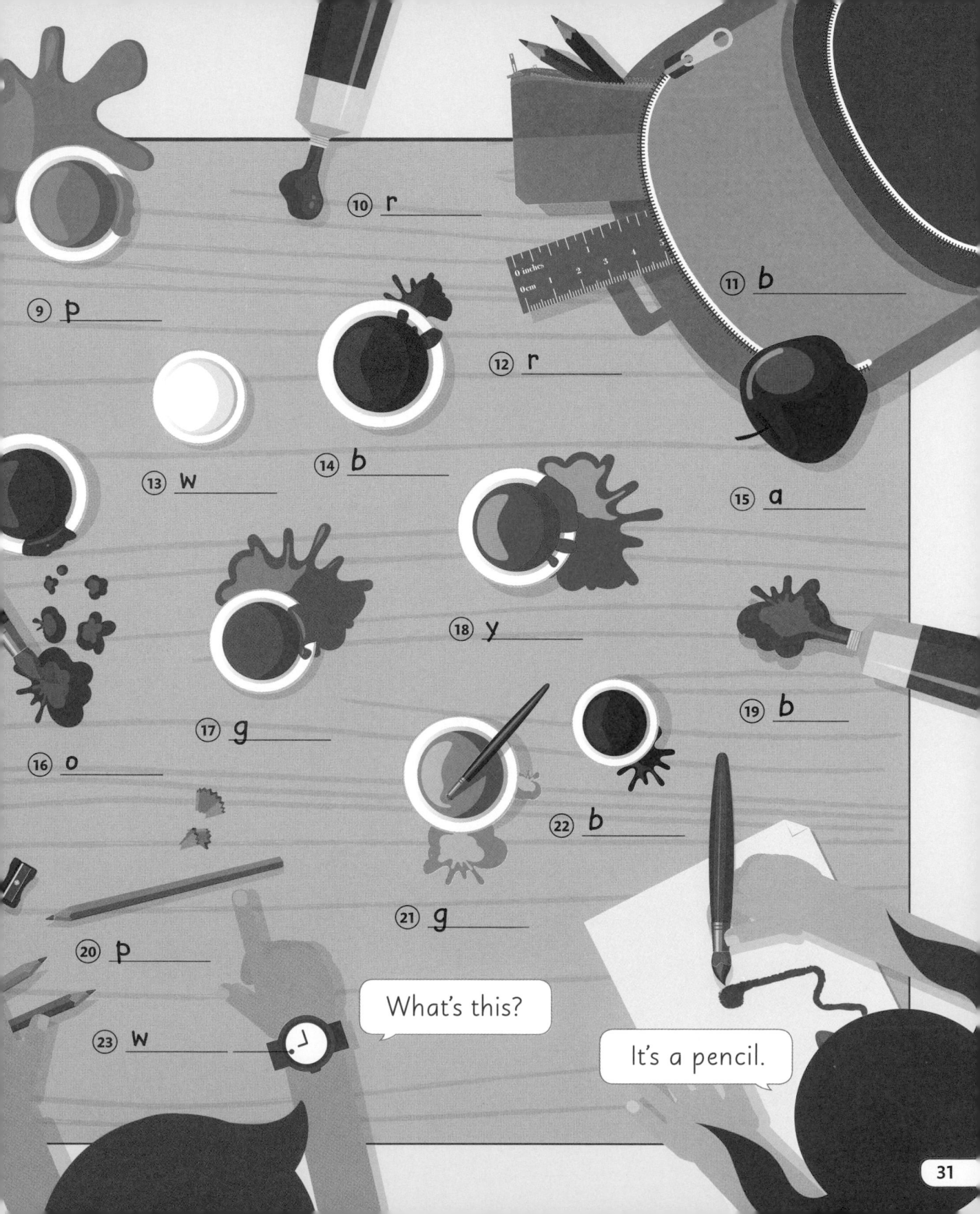
9 p
10 r
11 b
12 r
13 w
14 b
15 a
16 o
17 g
18 y
19 b
20 p
21 g
22 b
23 w
What's this?
It's a pencil.

4.2 Match the pictures to the correct words.

eraser

1 

ruler

2 

pencil

3 

watch

4 

crayon

5 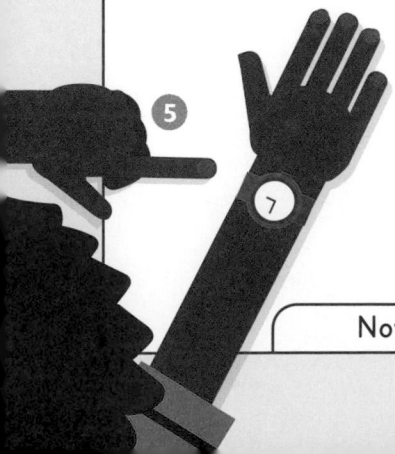

pen

Now listen and repeat.

4.3 Write the correct words next to the pictures.

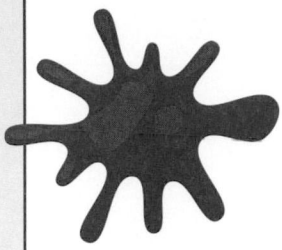

r e d

1 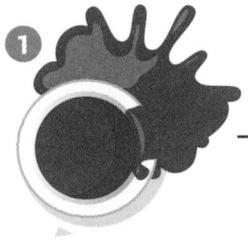

_ _ _ _ _

2 

_ _ _ _

3 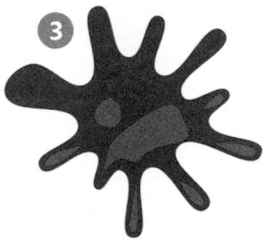

_ _ _ _ _

4 

_ _ _ _ _

5 

_ _ _ _

Now listen and repeat.

4.4 Look at the pictures and check off the correct words.

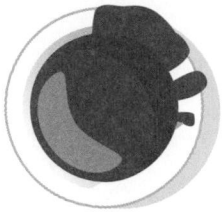

- white ☐
- blue ☑
- pink ☐

1

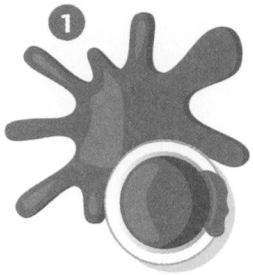

- purple ☐
- green ☐
- crayon ☐

2

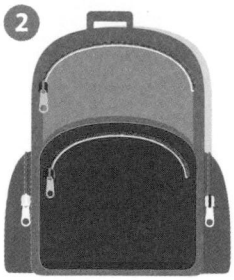

- watch ☐
- ruler ☐
- book pack ☐

3

- paper ☐
- white ☐
- watch ☐

4

- pink ☐
- notepad ☐
- red ☐

5

- orange ☐
- blue ☐
- apple ☐

6

- red ☐
- crayon ☐
- yellow ☐

7

- paper ☐
- brown ☐
- pencil ☐

Now listen and repeat.

4.5 Listen and check off the correct pictures.

A ☑ B ☐

1 A ☐ B ☐

2 A ☐ B ☐

3 A ☐ B ☐

4 A ☐ B ☐

5 A ☐ B ☐

4.6 Look at the pictures and write the correct answers in the spaces.

It's a ball. ~~They're books.~~
It's a watch. They're rulers.

What are these?

They're books.

1 What's this?

_____

2 What's this?

_____

3 What are these?

_____

Now listen and repeat.

4.7 Look at the pictures and write the correct words in the spaces.

It's | What are | They're | ~~What's~~ | these | apple

Now listen and repeat.

4.8 Listen to the song and color in the picture.

Red,
yellow,
green,
and blue!

Black
white, and
orange, too!

4.9 Listen and check off the correct pictures.

A ☐ B ☑

1. A ☐ B ☐
2. A ☐ B ☐
3. A ☐ B ☐
4. A ☐ B ☐

4.10 Look at the picture and match the questions to the correct answers.

What color is the book?

It's red.

1. What color is the book pack?

It's blue.

2. What color is the apple?

It's orange.

3. What color is the ball?

It's purple.

Now listen and repeat.

5 Our favorite animals

5.1 Listen and write the correct words in the spaces.

12 p
13 b
14 w
15 p
16 c
17 l
It's a crocodile!
What's that?
lion
hippo
~~zebra~~
elephant
giraffe
tiger
bear
monkey
parrot
snake
frog
whale
polar bear
bird
crocodile
lizard
penguin

5.2 Look at the pictures and circle the correct words.

giraffe / frog

1 hippo / polar bear

2 lion / parrot

3 tiger / snake

4 bear / elephant

5 crocodile / bird

Now listen and repeat.

5.3 Find and circle the five words in the grid.

bear
lizard
~~snake~~
whale
frog
bird

w	s	f	r	o	g
h	g	a	s	l	v
a	b	w	n	z	x
l	i	z	a	r	d
e	r	y	k	c	k
f	d	b	e	a	r

5.4 Look at the pictures and write the letters in the correct order.

s a k n e

s n a k e

1

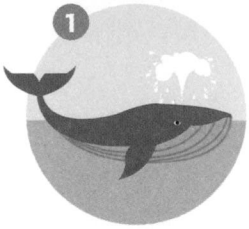

w l h a e

w _ _ _ _

2

l o n i

l _ _ _

3

z b a e r

z _ _ _ _

4

b r a e

b _ _ _

Now listen and repeat.

5.5 Listen to the song and write the correct words in the spaces.

Animals, animals
everywhere!
A lion, a giraffe,
and a _____.

A _____ and
a _____,
a tiger and a _____,
animals, animals,
they are great!

5.6 Look at the pictures and write the correct words in the spaces.

What's | that | They're | ~~frog~~

What's that?

It's a frog.

1 What's _____ ?

It's a polar bear.

2 What are those?

_____ hippos.

3 _____ that?

It's a snake.

Now listen and repeat.

5.7 Look at the pictures and write the correct answers in the spaces.

It's a crocodile. ~~They're monkeys.~~
They're parrots. It's a zebra.

What are those?

They're monkeys.

1 What's that?

_____

2 What's that?

_____

3 What are those?

_____

Now listen and repeat.

5.8 Listen and match the questions to the correct answers.

What are those?

1 What's that?

2 What are those?

3 What's that?

4 What are those?

5 What's that?

It's a lizard.

It's a bird.

They're elephants.

They're lions.

It's a parrot.

They're penguins.

5.9 There are four sentences. Mark the beginning and end of each one and write them below.

Whatarethose?|They'retigers.What'sthat?It'sanelephant.

What are those? _____

1 _____

2 _____

3 _____

Now listen and repeat.

5.10 Listen and check off the correct pictures.

A ☐ B ☑

1 

A ☐ B ☐

2 

A ☐ B ☐

3 

A ☐ B ☐

4 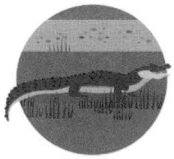

A ☐ B ☐

5 

A ☐ B ☐

5.11 Look at the pictures and write the correct words in the spaces.

bird ~~frog~~ monkey bear elephant lizard

What's your favorite animal?

My favorite animal is a frog.

1 

What's your favorite animal?

My favorite animal is a _____.

2 

What's your favorite animal?

My favorite animal is a _____.

3 

What's your favorite animal?

My favorite animal is a _____.

4 

What's your favorite animal?

My favorite animal is an _____.

5 

What's your favorite animal?

My favorite animal is a _____.

Now listen and repeat.

6 This is my family

6.1 Listen and write the correct words in the spaces.

① my family

② my g

③ my g

④ my f

⑤ my m

⑥ my b

⑦ my s

⑧ me

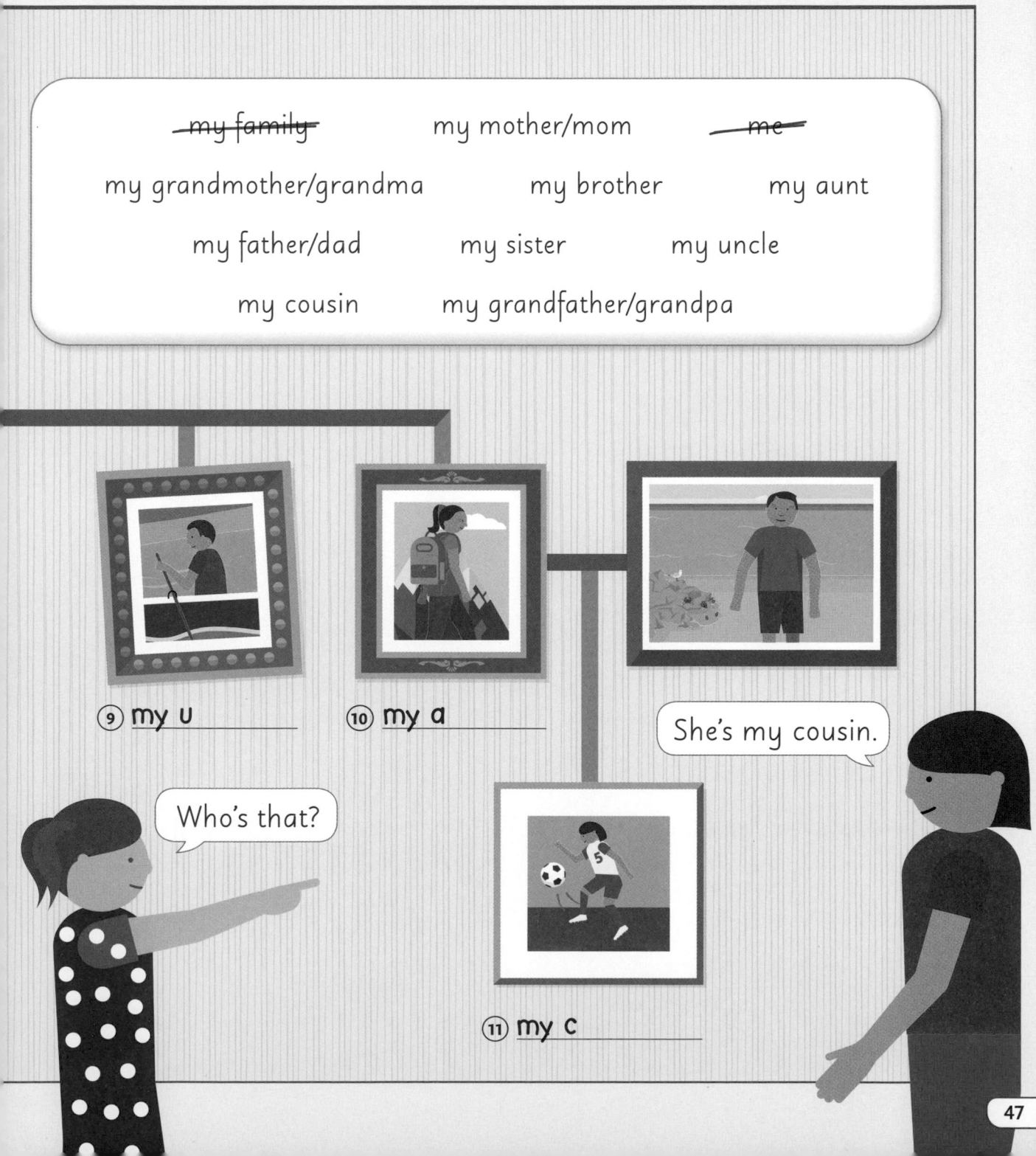
~~my family~~
my mother/mom
~~me~~
my grandmother/grandma
my brother
my aunt
my father/dad
my sister
my uncle
my cousin
my grandfather/grandpa
9 my u
10 my a
11 my c
Who's that?
She's my cousin.

6.2 Match the pictures to the correct words.

my cousin

my dad

my uncle

my grandma

my grandpa

my family

Now listen and repeat.

6.3 Look at the pictures and check off the correct words.

- aunt ☑
- uncle ☐
- grandmother ☐

- sister ☐
- aunt ☐
- brother ☐

- cousin ☐
- mother ☐
- father ☐

- grandma ☐
- sister ☐
- grandfather ☐

- sister ☐
- grandpa ☐
- uncle ☐

Now listen and repeat.

6.4 Look at the pictures and write the correct words in the spaces.

grandma ~~brother~~ uncle cousin sister dad

Who's this? He's my brother.

1 Who's this? She's my _____.

2 Who's that? He's my _____.

3 Who's this? She's my _____.

4 Who's that? He's my _____.

5 Who's this? She's my _____.

Now listen and repeat.

6.5 Listen and check off the correct answers.

Is he your dad?

- Yes, he is. ☑
- No, he isn't. ☐

1. Is he your brother?

- Yes, he is. ☐
- No, he isn't. ☐

2. Is she your sister?

- Yes, she is. ☐
- No, she isn't. ☐

3. Is she your mother?

- Yes, she is. ☐
- No, she isn't. ☐

6.6 Match the pictures to the correct words.

1 2 3 4

chef firefighter vet doctor teacher

Now listen and repeat.

6.7 Find and circle the four words in the grid.

teacher vet ~~doctor~~ farmer chef

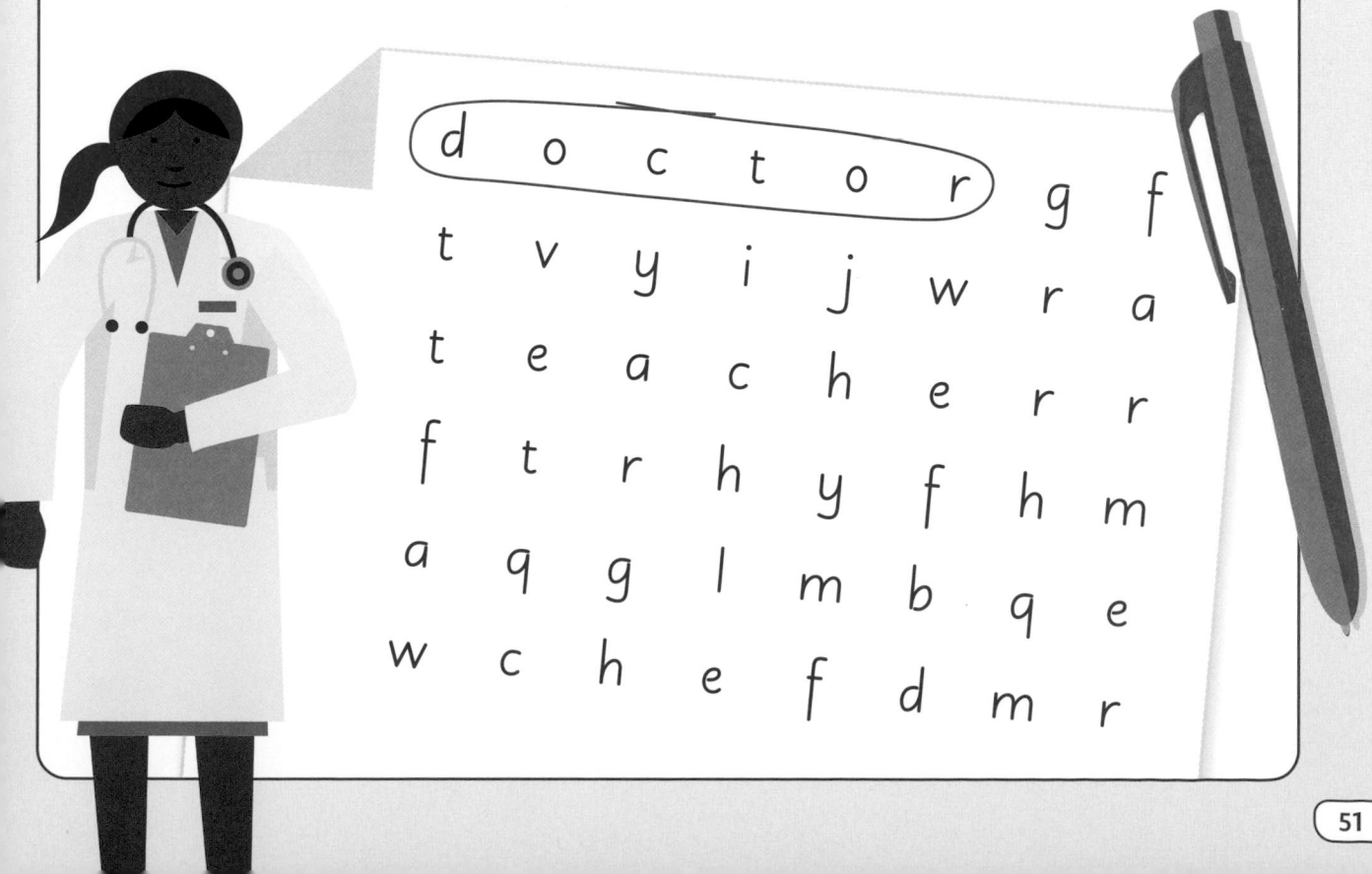

d	o	c	t	o	r	g	f
t	v	y	i	j	w	r	a
t	e	a	c	h	e	r	r
f	t	r	h	y	f	h	m
a	q	g	l	m	b	q	e
w	c	h	e	f	d	m	r

6.8 Look at the pictures and write the correct words in the spaces.

teacher ~~farmer~~ chef
doctor police officer

He's a farmer.

1 She's a _____.

2 He's a _____.

3 She's a _____.

4 She's a _____.

Now listen and repeat.

6.9 Look at the pictures and check off the correct sentences.

He's a firefighter. ☑
She's a firefighter. ☐

He's a doctor. ☐
She's a doctor. ☐

She's a chef. ☐
He's a chef. ☐

He's a farmer. ☐
She's a farmer. ☐

He's a teacher. ☐
She's a teacher. ☐

She's a police officer. ☐
He's a police officer. ☐

Now listen and repeat.

6.10 Listen to the song and write the correct words in the spaces.

Who's this?
She's my mother .
Who's that?
He's my _____ .

My _____ is a teacher,
my _____ is a vet,
Grandpa's a _____ ,
and Grandma's a _____ !

7 This is my room

13 b
14 t
15 b
16 b
17 s
18 t
lamp
computer
desk
~~poster~~
keyboard
toy box
rug
mouse
doll
car
bed
chair
skateboard
camera
baseball bat
tennis racket
teddy bear
ball

7.2 Match the pictures to the correct words.

skateboard

1 

doll

2 

car

3 

lamp

4 

chair

5 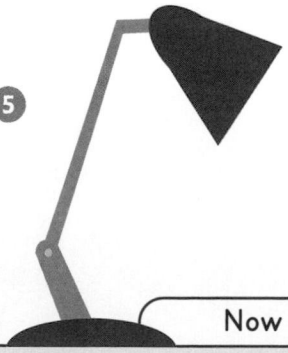

toy box

Now listen and repeat.

7.3 Listen and check off the correct pictures.

A ☐

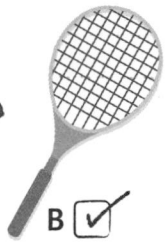

B ☑

1 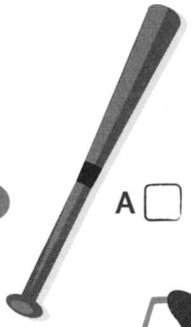

A ☐

B ☐

2 

A ☐

B ☐

3 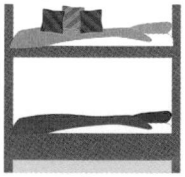

A ☐

B ☐

4 

A ☐

B ☐

7.4 Read the sentences and check off the correct pictures.

This is my teddy bear.

A ☐ B ☑

1 These are my cars.

A ☐ B ☐

2 This is my camera.

A ☐ B ☐

3 This is my computer.

A ☐ B ☐

4 These are my dolls.

A ☐ B ☐

5 This is my ball.

A ☐ B ☐

Now listen and repeat.

7.5 Listen and match the names to the correct pictures.

Ben

1 Anna

2 Jack

3 Emma

4 Harry

car

computer

doll

skateboard

toy box

7.6 Look at the pictures and write the correct words in the spaces.

Those are | That's | ~~This is~~ | That's
This is | These are

_____This is_____ my doll.

1 _____ my ball.

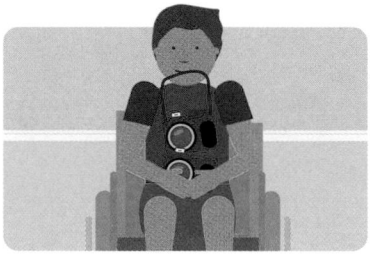

2 _____ my cameras.

3 _____ my teddy bears.

4 _____ my toy box.

5 _____ my tennis racket.

Now listen and repeat.

7.7 Look at the pictures and write the correct names in the spaces.

Maria

Andy

I have a computer.

Maria

1 I have a rug.

_____

2 I don't have a doll.

_____

3 I don't have a chair.

_____

4 I have a skateboard.

_____

5 I don't have a lamp.

_____

6 I have a teddy bear.

_____

7 I don't have a car.

_____

Now listen and repeat.

7.8 Listen and write the correct answers below.

Yes, I do. ~~No, I don't.~~ No, I don't.
No, I don't. Yes, I do.

Do you have a baseball bat?

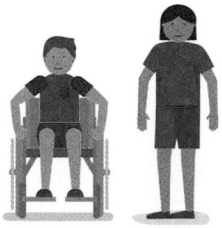

No, I don't.

1. Do you have a car?

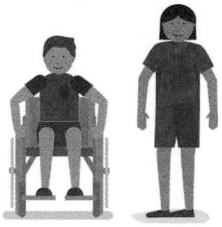

_____

2. Do you have a chair?

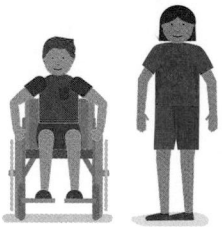

_____

3. Do you have a lamp?

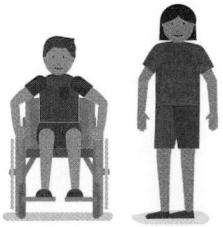

_____

4. Do you have a desk?

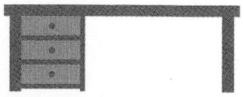

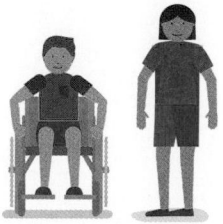

_____

7.9 Look at the pictures and check off the correct answers.

Do you have a car?

Yes, I do. ☐

No, I don't. ☑

1 Do you have a rug?

Yes, I do. ☐

No, I don't. ☐

2 Do you have a ball?

Yes, I do. ☐

No, I don't. ☐

3 Do you have a poster?

Yes, I do. ☐

No, I don't. ☐

4 Do you have a doll?

Yes, I do. ☐

No, I don't. ☐

5 Do you have a desk?

Yes, I do. ☐

No, I don't. ☐

Now listen and repeat.

7.10 Listen to the song and write the correct words in the spaces.

This is my toy box

and these are my _____ ,

I have a _____

and a _____ , too.

Toys are fantastic!

Toys are cool!

8 Review: This is me

8.1 Listen and read.

My name's Max.
I'm ten years old.
My favorite animal is a hippo.
I have a tablet.
I don't have a computer.

My favorite toy is my ball.

8.2 Write about yourself then draw your room and your favorite toy.

My name's _____.

I'm _____ years old.

My favorite animal is _____.

I have a _____.

I don't have a _____.

My favorite toy is my _____.

9 At the fair

9.1 Listen and write the correct words in the spaces.

hungry
~~tired~~
thirsty
cold
scared
hot
happy
excited
sad

① tired

② h

③ t

4 s
5 h
6 c
7 e
8 s
9 h

9.2 Look at the pictures and circle the correct words.

excited / tired

cold / hungry

scared / excited

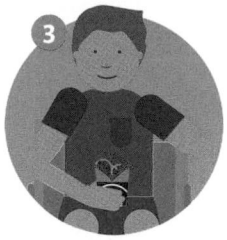

thirsty / hungry

sad / tired

happy / hot

Now listen and repeat.

9.3 Listen and check off the correct pictures.

A ☐

B ☑

1 A ☐

B ☐

2 A ☐ B ☐

3 A ☐

B ☐

4 A ☐

B ☐

5 A ☐

B ☐

9.4 Look at the pictures and write the correct words next to the pictures.

happy ~~cold~~ tired
excited thirsty

cold _____

1 

_____

2 

_____

3 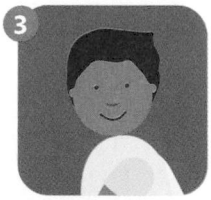

_____

4 

_____

Now listen and repeat.

9.5 Listen to the song and write the correct words in the spaces.

Are you __happy__ ?
_____ , we are!
We are at the fair.

Are you _____ ?
_____ , we aren't.
We aren't tired
or _____ !

9.6 Match the pictures to the correct sentences.

We're thirsty. We're very scared. We're really hot. We're happy.

Now listen and repeat.

9.7 Listen and check off the correct sentences.

We're excited. ☑
They're excited. ☐

We're happy. ☐
They're happy. ☐

We're cold. ☐
They're cold. ☐

We're hot. ☐
They're hot. ☐

We're sad. ☐
They're sad. ☐

We're thirsty. ☐
They're thirsty. ☐

We're tired. ☐
They're tired. ☐

We're scared. ☐
They're scared. ☐

9.8 Look at the pictures and write the correct words in the spaces.

hot ~~thirsty~~ really happy excited

They're very thirsty .

1 We're really _____ .

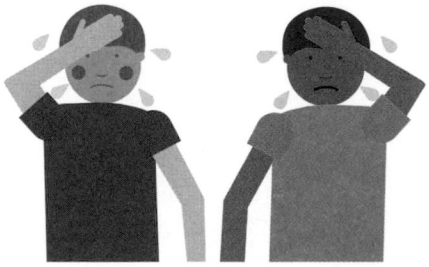

2 They're _____ .

3 We're _____ .

4 We're _____ tired.

Now listen and repeat.

9.9 Look at the pictures and check off the correct answers.

Are they excited?

Yes, they are. ☐

No, they're not. ☑

1 Are you scared?

Yes, we are. ☐

No, we're not. ☐

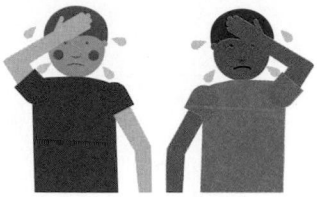

2 Are you hot?

Yes, we are. ☐

No, we're not. ☐

3 Are they cold?

Yes, they are. ☐

No, they're not. ☐

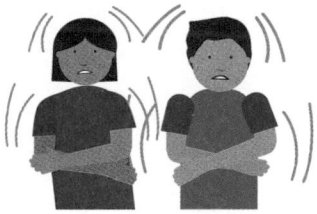

4 Are you tired?

Yes, we are. ☐

No, we're not. ☐

5 Are they sad?

Yes, they are. ☐

No, they're not. ☐

Now listen and repeat.

9.10 Listen and match the questions to the correct answers.

Are you sad? — Yes, they are.

1 Are they happy? — No, we're not.

2 Are you excited? — No, they're not.

3 Are you hungry? — No, we're not.

4 Are they scared? — Yes, we are.

9.11 Look at the pictures and write the correct answers in the spaces.

No, we're not. Yes, they are. ~~Yes, we are.~~ No, they're not.
Yes, they are. No, we're not. No, they're not. Yes, we are.

Are you cold?

Yes, we are.

1 Are they hungry?

_____

2 Are you happy?

_____

3 Are they thirsty?

_____

4 Are they excited?

_____

5 Are you scared?

_____

6 Are you excited?

_____

7 Are they happy?

_____

Now listen and repeat.

10 Our pets

10.1 Listen and write the correct words in the spaces.
dog
collar
~~rabbit~~
mouse
tortoise
vet
spider
cat
fish
Look! Andy has a dog.
Yes, it's very dirty.
1 rabbit
2 t
3 d
4 m
5 c

6 S
7 C
8 V
9 f

10.2 Look at the pictures and write the correct words in the spaces.

scary ~~young~~ dirty old big
nice small clean beautiful

young

1 o

2 n

3 s

4 d

5 c

6 b

7 b

8 s

Now listen and repeat.

10.3 Look at the pictures and check off the correct words.

cat ☐
tortoise ☑

1
dog ☐
rabbit ☐

2
fish ☐
rabbit ☐

3
spider ☐
vet ☐

4
cat ☐
collar ☐

Now listen and repeat.

10.4 Look at the pictures and write the correct words.

vet ~~fish~~ dog mouse tortoise cat

fish

1 _____

2 _____

3 _____

4 _____

5 _____

Now listen and repeat.

10.5 Listen and check off the correct pictures.

A ☐ B ☑

1 A ☐ B ☐

2 A ☐ B ☐

3 A ☐ B ☐

4 A ☐ B ☐

10.6 Listen to the song and write the correct words in the spaces.

I have a ___cat___ ,
she's _____ and _____ .
She likes to run
and play with a ball.

Maria has a _____ ,
his name is Socks.
He's _____ and _____
and he's in this box.

10.7 Match the pictures to the correct words.

Ben has a rabbit.

He has a mouse.

She has a fish.

Sara has a tortoise.

He has a cat.

She has a cat.

Now listen and repeat.

10.8 Listen and check off the correct pictures.

A ☐ B ☑

1 A ☐ B ☐

2 A ☐ B ☐

3 A ☐ B ☐

4 A ☐ B ☐

5 A ☐ B ☐

10.9 Look at the pictures and check off the correct answers.

Does she have a dog?

- Yes, she does. ☐
- No, she doesn't. ☑

1. Does he have a cat?

- Yes, he does. ☐
- No, he doesn't. ☐

2. Does she have a tortoise?

- Yes, she does. ☐
- No, she doesn't. ☐

3. Does he have a spider?

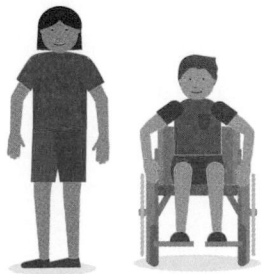

- Yes, he does. ☐
- No, he doesn't. ☐

Now listen and repeat.

10.10 Read the questions and check off the correct pictures.

Which dog is clean?

A ☑ B ☐

1 Which one is nice?

A ☐ B ☐

2 Which dog is small?

A ☐ B ☐

3 Which one is young?

A ☐ B ☐

4 Which dog is dirty?

A ☐ B ☐

5 Which one is old?

A ☐ B ☐

Now listen and repeat.

10.11 There are four sentences. Mark the beginning and end of each one and write them below.

Which pet is small?

1 _____

2 _____

3 _____

Whichpetissmall? Themouse.Whichoneisscary?Thespider!

Now listen and repeat.

11 My body

11.1 Listen and write the correct words in the spaces.

body nose mouth face ~~hair~~ arm
hand toes long hair foot leg feet fingers
head ear short hair teeth eye
The robot has red eyes.
14 h
15 s
16 e
17 e
18 t

11.2 Find and circle the five words in the grid.

teeth fingers ~~leg~~ hair feet arm

d	g	f	l	b	x	a
t	e	e	t	h	h	r
r	l	e	g	n	a	m
j	k	t	k	b	i	f
f	i	n	g	e	r	s

11.3 Match the pictures to the correct words.

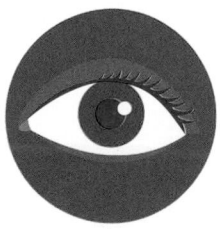

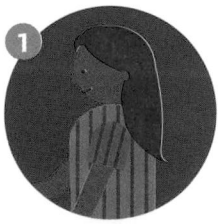

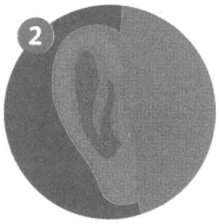

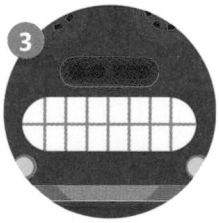

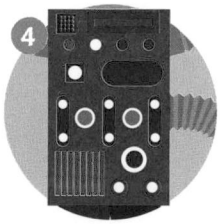

ear eye body long hair teeth

Now listen and repeat.

11.4 Write the correct words next to the pictures.

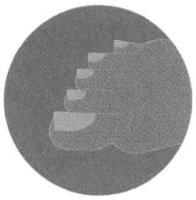

t o e s

1 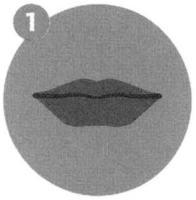

_ _ _ _ _

2 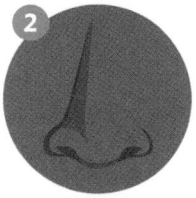

_ _ _ _

3 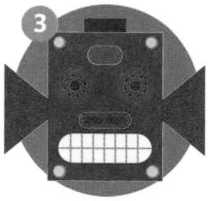

_ _ _ _

4 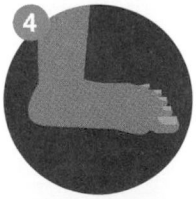

_ _ _ _

5 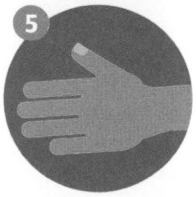

_ _ _ _

Now listen and repeat.

11.5 Listen and check off the correct pictures.

A ☐

B ☑

1 

A ☐

B ☐

2 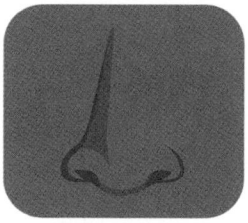

A ☐

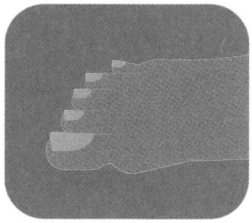

B ☐

3 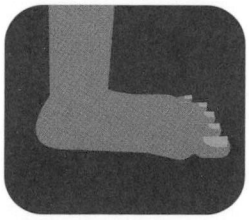

A ☐

B ☐

11.6 Look at the picture and write the correct words in the spaces.

legs purple ~~ears~~ teeth
hands yellow blue

The robot has green ears .

1. The robot has _____ eyes.
2. It has red _____ .
3. It has purple _____ .
4. The robot has _____ feet.
5. It has a _____ nose.
6. The robot has orange _____ .

Now listen and repeat.

11.7 Listen and color in the robot.

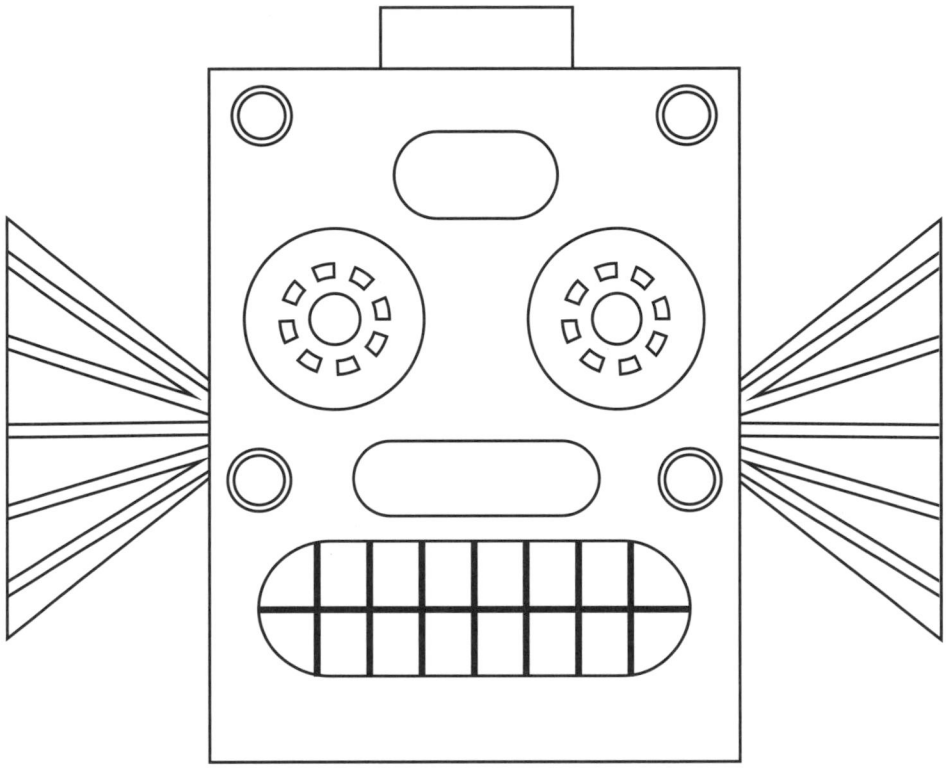

11.8 Listen and circle the correct answers.

Does the robot have four arms?

Yes, it does. / No, it doesn't.

1. Does it have black feet?

   Yes, it does. / No, it doesn't.

2. Does it have green eyes?

   Yes, it does. / No, it doesn't.

3. Does the robot have orange teeth?

   Yes, it does. / No, it doesn't.

4. Does the robot have two legs?

   Yes, it does. / No, it doesn't.

5. Does it have purple toes?

   Yes, it does. / No, it doesn't.

11.9 Look at the picture and write the correct answers in the spaces.

No, it doesn't. ~~Yes, it does.~~ Yes, it does.
Yes, it does. No, it doesn't. Yes, it does.

Does it have three arms?

Yes, it does.

1. Does it have purple eyes?

_____

2. Does it have two legs?

_____

3. Does it have orange hands?

_____

4. Does it have blue ears?

_____

5. Does it have three hands?

_____

Now listen and repeat.

11.10 Match the pictures to the correct words.

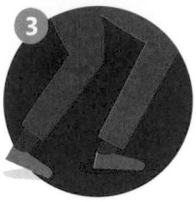

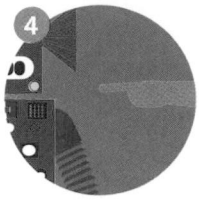

touch point wave clap move

Now listen and repeat.

11.11 Listen to the song and write the correct words in the spaces.

Clap your hands,
_____ your nose,
_____ your feet,
_____ your toes!

Point one _____ ,
move your head,
_____ your arms,
touch one leg!

12 Our town

12.1 Listen and write the correct words in the spaces.
park airplane
train ~~airport~~ lake
bookstore zoo
street boat bike
fire station house
school helicopter
apartment block
store hospital
bus truck
motorcycle car
1 airport
2 a
3 s
4 t
5 b
6 z
7 p
8 b
ZOO
BOOKS
Café
Where do you live?
I live next to the fire station.

9 l
10 b
11 h
12 s
13 f
14 a
15 h
16 h
BOOKS
TOYS
17 s
18 t
19 c
20 b
21 m

12.2 Look at the pictures and circle the correct words.

zoo / street

bus / truck

house / school

bike / helicopter

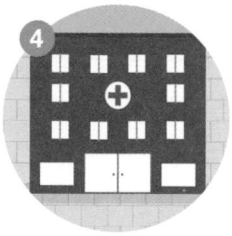

hospital / store

park / truck

Now listen and repeat.

12.3 Listen and check off the correct pictures.

A ☑ B ☐

1 A ☐ B ☐

2 A ☐ B ☐

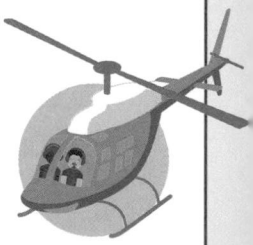

3 A ☐ B ☐

4 A ☐ B ☐

5 A ☐ B ☐

12.4 Look at the pictures and write the letters in the correct order.

h u s e o

h o u s e

1

c r a

c _ _

2

t a i r n

t _ _ _ _

3

l k a e

l _ _ _

4

p r k a

p _ _ _

Now listen and repeat.

12.5 Listen to the song and write the correct words in the spaces.

This is my town,
there's a park
and a _____ .
There's an _____ ,
a _____ , and
a fire station, too.

This is my town,
there are _____ and
a _____ .
This is my town,
I love it, it's cool.

12.6 Look at the pictures and write the correct words in the spaces.

There are ~~There's~~ There are There's There are There's

There's a lake.

1 _____ two stores.

2 _____ a fire station.

3 _____ a zoo.

4 _____ three houses.

5 _____ four cars.

Now listen and repeat.

12.7 Read the sentences and check off the correct pictures.

There are two motorcycles.

A ☐ B ☑

1 There's a car.

A ☐ B ☐

2 There are four bikes.

A ☐ B ☐

3 There are three boats.

A ☐ B ☐

4 There's a house.

A ☐ B ☐

5 There's a truck.

A ☐ B ☐

Now listen and repeat.

12.8 Look at the pictures and check off the correct words.

behind ☑
next to ☐
in front of ☐

1

between ☐
in front of ☐
behind ☐

2

between ☐
next to ☐
in front of ☐

3

behind ☐
between ☐
next to ☐

Now listen and repeat.

12.9 Look at the picture and write the correct words in the spaces.

Where's the bike?
It's next to the bookstore.

1. Where's the bookstore?
It's _____ the green car.

2. Where's the school?
It's _____ the lake.

3. Where's the fire station?
It's _____ the school.

4. Where's the house?
It's _____ the hospital and the bookstore.

5. Where's the bus?
It's _____ the hospital.

in front of ~~next to~~ behind in front of next to between

Now listen and repeat.

12.10 Listen and match the questions to the correct answers.

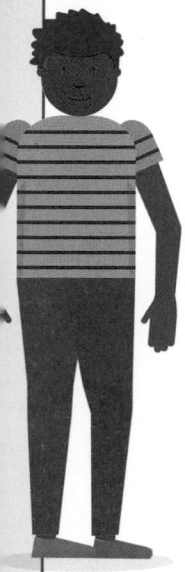

Where do you live?

1. Where's the park?
2. Where's the truck?
3. Where's the zoo?
4. Where's the lake?
5. Where's the school?

It's behind the hospital.

It's between the fire station and the store.

It's behind the school.

I live in front of the zoo.

It's between the airport and the apartment block.

It's next to the lake.

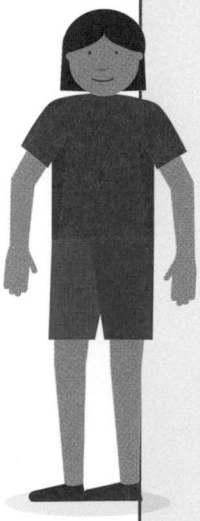

I live next to the zoo.

And you?

I live _____

_____

13 My home

13.1 Listen and write the correct words in the spaces.

plants bedroom
clock ~~garden~~
television/TV
couch bath floor
living room wall
door window kitchen
mat refrigerator
armchair dining room
bookcase hall chair
mirror lights table
bathroom flowers

① garden

② b

③ c

④ p

⑬ l

⑭ t

⑮ c

Where's Sara?

She's in the bedroom.

5 w
6 w
7 f
8 a
9 b
10 b
11 m
12 b
16 h
17 d
18 m
19 l
20 k
21 r
22 d
23 f
24 t
25 c

13.2 Look at the pictures and circle the correct words.

kitchen / bathroom

dining room / bathroom

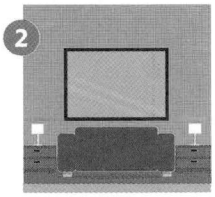

bedroom / living room

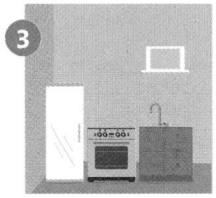

kitchen / living room

bedroom / dining room

kitchen / hall

Now listen and repeat.

13.3 Match the pictures to the correct words.

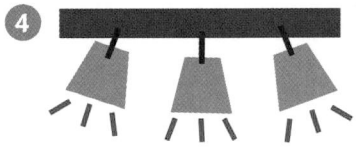

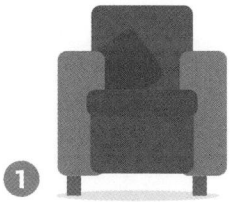

table television lights armchair window

Now listen and repeat.

13.4 Look at the pictures and check off the correct words.

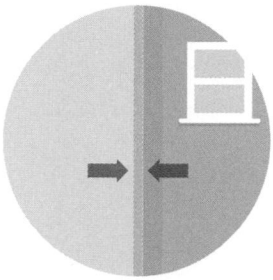

- table ☐
- wall ☑
- television ☐

1

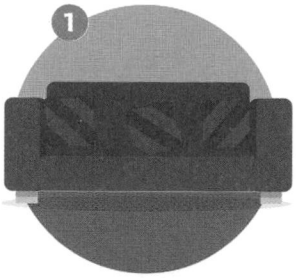

- couch ☐
- floor ☐
- flowers ☐

2

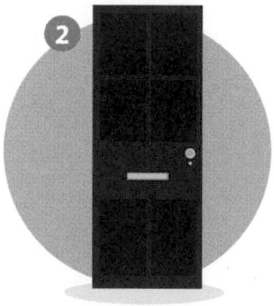

- clock ☐
- television ☐
- door ☐

3

- bookcase ☐
- refrigerator ☐
- mirror ☐

Now listen and repeat.

13.5 Look at the pictures and write the correct words in the spaces.

bookcase ~~door~~
clock plants chair

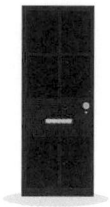

door _____

1  _____

2  _____

3  _____

4  _____

Now listen and repeat.

13.6 Write the correct words under the pictures.

under ~~in~~ on

i n

1 ___ ___

2 ___ ___ ___ ___ ___

Now listen and repeat.

13.7 Look at the pictures and circle the correct words.

The book is
(on) / **under** the floor.

The cat is
in / **on** the bath.

The plants are
on / **under** the window.

The cat is
on / **in** the mat.

The bookcase is
under / **on** the lights.

The flowers are
in / **on** the table.

Now listen and repeat.

13.8 Listen and check off the correct pictures.

A ☐

B ☑

1 A ☐

B ☐

2 A ☐

B ☐

3 A ☐

B ☐

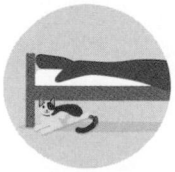

4 A ☐

B ☐

13.9 Listen to the song and write the correct words in the spaces.

♪ ♪

♪ The TV's ___in___
the living room,
the _____ is in the _____ .

Where's the _____ ?
It's _____ my
bedroom _____ .

♪

13.10 Look at the pictures and write the correct answers in the spaces.

Yes, there is.	~~Is there~~	No, there isn't.
No, there isn't.	Yes, there is.	Is there

1 Is there a couch in the kitchen?

_____

2 Is there a bookcase in the bedroom?

_____

3 Is there a clock in the bathroom?

_____

4 Is there a window in the bedroom?

_____

5 _____ a table in the dining room?

Yes, there is.

Now listen and repeat.

13.11 Look at the picture and write the correct answers in the spaces.

Yes, there are. ~~Yes, there are.~~ No, there aren't.
No, there aren't. No, there aren't. Yes, there are.

Are there any plants in the garden?

Yes, there are.

1 Are there any flowers in the kitchen?

_____

2 Are there any windows in the dining room?

_____

3 Are there any clocks in the bedroom?

_____

4 Are there any chairs in the dining room?

_____

5 Are there any armchairs in the living room?

_____

Now listen and repeat.

14 Review: Where I live

14.1 Listen and read.

I'm Andy and this is my town.

In my town, there's a hospital and a school.
There are two parks and three stores.

That's my house. I live next to the hospital.

14.2 Write about your town then draw your house and town.

I'm _____ and this is my town.

In my town, there's a _____ and a _____. There are _____ and _____.

That's my house. I live _____ the _____.

15 On the farm

barn
tree
~~pig~~
sheep
pond
tractor
chicken
duck
field
donkey
the sun
goat
cow
horse
bee
tail

15.2 Find and circle the five words in the grid.

tail donkey ~~barn~~
pig bee horse

g	t	d	i	h	b
b	a	r	n	o	e
p	i	g	l	r	e
r	l	e	w	s	i
d	o	n	k	e	y

15.3 Listen and check off the correct pictures.

A ☐ B ☑

1 

A ☐ B ☐

2 

A ☐ B ☐

3 A ☐ B ☐

4 A ☐ B ☐

5 A ☐ B ☐

15.4 Look at the pictures and circle the correct words.

bee / goat

1 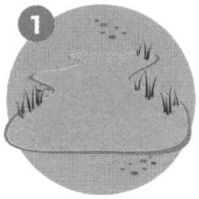

donkey / pond

2 

sheep / tractor

3 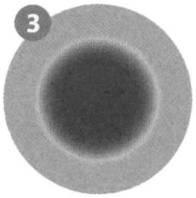

the sun / horse

4 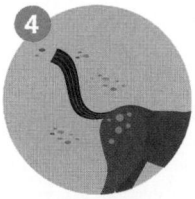

duck / tail

5 

tree / chicken

Now listen and repeat.

15.5 Look at the pictures and write the correct words in the spaces.

barn goat ~~chicken~~
donkey field sheep

chicken

1  _____

2  _____

3  _____

4  _____

5  _____

Now listen and repeat.

15.6 Look at the picture and match the questions to the correct answers.

How many barns are there?	There are five.
1 How many sheep are there?	There are three.
2 How many cows are there?	There are six.
3 How many goats are there?	There's one.
4 How many bees are there?	There are two.
5 How many chickens are there?	There are four.
6 How many donkeys are there?	There are seven.

Now listen and repeat.

15.7 Look at the pictures and circle the correct words.

How many ducks are there?

There's / There are two.

1 How many donkeys are there?

There's / There are three.

2 How many horses are there?

There's / There are one.

3 How many cows are there?

There's / There are four.

4 How many tractors are there?

There's / There are one.

Now listen and repeat.

15.8 Look at the pictures and write the correct words in the spaces.

behind ~~in~~ next to in front of

Where are the cows?

They're in the field.

1 Where's the horse?

It's _____ the tree.

2 Where's the donkey?

It's _____ the pond.

3 Where are the goats?

They're _____ the barn.

Now listen and repeat.

15.9 Listen to the song and write the correct words in the spaces.

Where are the ___ducks___ ?
They're in the _____ !

Where are the _____ ?
They're _____ the field!

Where are the _____ ?
They're in the _____ !

_____ are the animals?
They're _____ my farm!

15.10 Look at the pictures and check off the correct sentences.

The donkey's in the field. ☑
The donkeys are in the field. ☐

The duck's in the pond. ☐
The ducks are in the pond. ☐

The sheep's in front of the barn. ☐
The sheep are in front of the barn. ☐

The horse is under the tree. ☐
The horses are under the tree. ☐

Now listen and repeat.

16 Sports

16.1 Listen and write the correct words in the spaces.

① basketball

② b

③ s

④ t

~~basketball~~ baseball

table tennis ice hockey

tennis soccer

swimming badminton

5 b
6 s
7 t
8 i

16.2 Write the correct words under the pictures.

b a s e b a l l

b _ _ _ _ _ _ _ _

t _ _ _ _ _

s _ _ _ _ _ _ _

Now listen and repeat.

16.3 Listen and check off the correct pictures.

A ☐

B ☑

1 

A ☐

B ☐

2 

A ☐

B ☐

3 A ☐

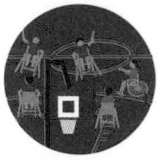

B ☐

4 

A ☐

B ☐

5 

A ☐

B ☐

16.4 Look at the pictures and write the correct words in the spaces.

swim play tennis ~~run~~ bounce throw
catch kick play ice hockey hit jump

run

1 j

2 s

3 p

4 p

5 c

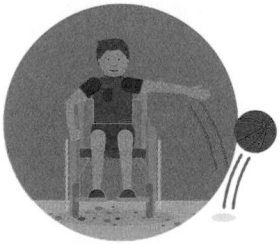

6 b

7 k

8 t

9 h

Now listen and repeat.

16.5 Look at the pictures and circle the correct words.

run / hit

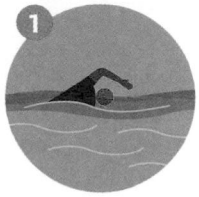

swim / run

jump / kick

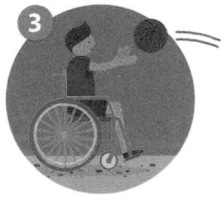

catch / bounce

throw / hit

Now listen and repeat.

16.6 Read the words and check off the correct pictures.

jump

A ☐

B ☑

1 play tennis

A ☐

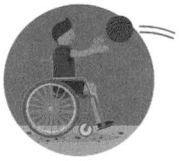

B ☐

2 run

A ☐

B ☐

3 bounce

A ☐

B ☐

4 play basketball

A ☐

B ☐

5 throw

A ☐

B ☐

Now listen and repeat.

16.7 Look at the pictures and write the correct words in the spaces.

jump catch ~~kick~~
throw bounce

kick

_____

_____

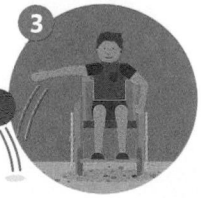

_____

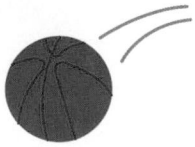

_____

Now listen and repeat.

16.8 Match the pictures to the correct words.

play soccer

play baseball

play tennis

play badminton

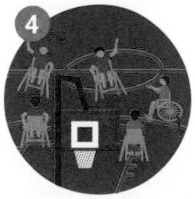

play ice hockey

play basketball

Now listen and repeat.

16.9 Listen and write the correct words in the spaces.

can't can ~~can't~~ can can't can can't

I can't play table tennis.

1 

I _____ play tennis.

2 

I _____ play baseball.

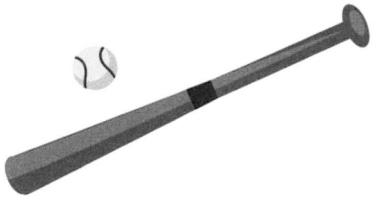

3 

I _____ play ice hockey.

4 

I _____ play basketball.

5 

I _____ play badminton.

6 

I _____ play soccer.

16.10 Listen and check off the correct answers.

Can you bounce a ball?

- [x] Yes, I can.
- [ ] No, I can't.

1. Can you swim?

- [ ] Yes, I can.
- [ ] No, I can't.

2. Can you play basketball?

- [ ] Yes, I can.
- [ ] No, I can't.

3. Can you throw a ball?

- [ ] Yes, I can.
- [ ] No, I can't.

4. Can you play soccer?

- [ ] Yes, I can.
- [ ] No, I can't.

16.11 Look at the pictures and write the correct words in the spaces.

she can | Can she | ~~he can't~~
Can he | she can't | he can

Can he play tennis?

No, he can't.

1 Can he catch a ball?

Yes, _____.

2 _____ run?

Yes, she can.

3 Can she play soccer?

No, _____.

4 Can she swim?

Yes, _____.

5 _____ play baseball?

No, he can't.

Now listen and repeat.

16.12 Listen and match the questions to the correct answers.

Can Max swim?	Yes, he can.
1 Can she play table tennis?	No, she can't.
2 Can Maria play badminton?	Yes, she can.
3 Can he play ice hockey?	No, he can't.

16.13 There are four sentences. Mark the beginning and end of each one and write them below.

Can she play baseball?

1 _____

2 _____

3 _____

Cansheplaybaseball?Yes,shecan.Canheswim?No,hecan't.

Now listen and repeat.

17 At the food market

oranges kiwis lemons limes

~~grapes~~ tomatoes mangoes pears

pineapples bananas meat coconuts

onions fruit watermelons potatoes

vegetables carrots fish apples

17.2 Look at the pictures and write the letters in the correct order.

o i n s n o

o n i o n s

k w i s i

1 k _ _ _ _

p r a e s

2 p _ _ _ _

a p l p s e

3 a _ _ _ _ _

f u t r i

4 f _ _ _ _

g p r a e s

5 g _ _ _ _ _

l m e s i

6 l _ _ _ _

m t a e

7 m _ _ _

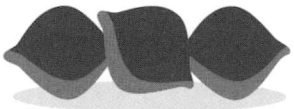

l m e n s o

8 l _ _ _ _ _

Now listen and repeat.

17.3 Match the pictures to the correct words.

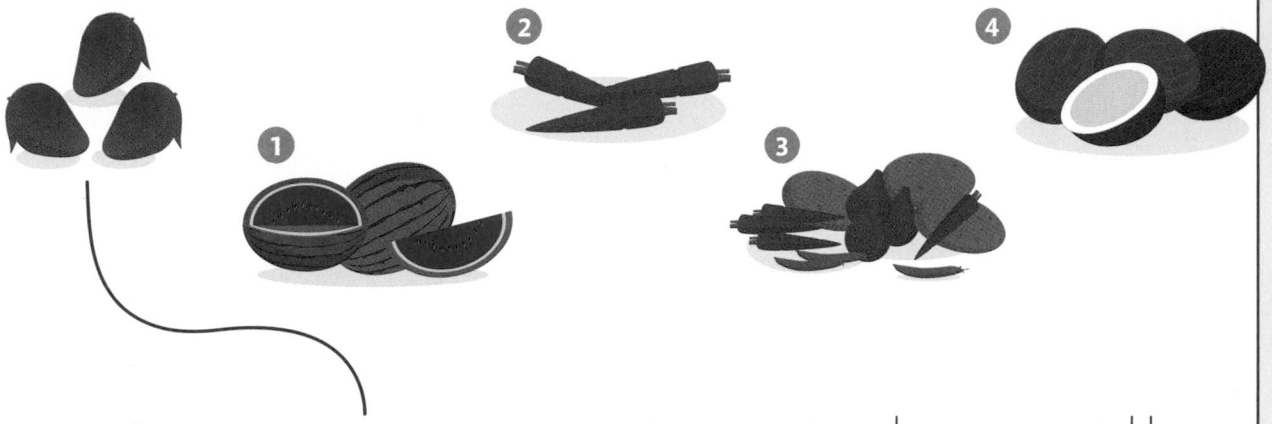

carrots mangoes coconuts watermelons vegetables

Now listen and repeat.

17.4 Listen to the song and write the correct words in the spaces.
17.5 Color in the three foods that you heard in the song.

Apples and oranges,
_____ and _____, too.
Here are nice _____,
and meat and _____ for you.

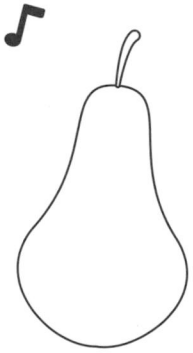

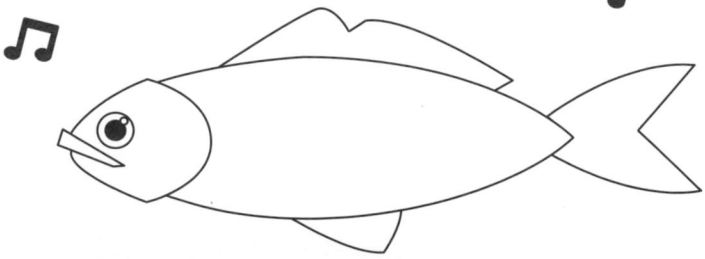

17.6 Look at the pictures and write the correct words in the spaces.

or ~~don't like~~ and like and or

I ___don't like___ pears or oranges.

1 I like tomatoes _____ carrots.

2 I don't like potatoes _____ onions.

3 I _____ lemons and limes.

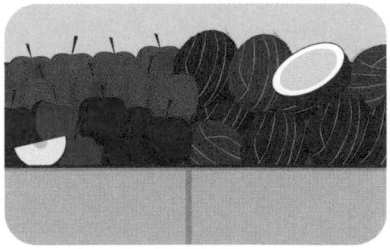

4 I don't like apples _____ coconuts.

5 I like mangoes _____ watermelons.

Now listen and repeat.

17.7 Listen and check off the correct answers.

Do you like pineapples?

- Yes, I do. ☑
- No, I don't. ☐

1. Do you like potatoes?

- Yes, I do. ☐
- No, I don't. ☐

2. Do you like grapes?

- Yes, I do. ☐
- No, I don't. ☐

3. Do you like meat?

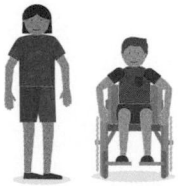

- Yes, I do. ☐
- No, I don't. ☐

4. Do you like bananas?

- Yes, I do. ☐
- No, I don't. ☐

17.8 Look at the pictures and circle the correct words.

May I have **an / some** apples, please?

1. May I have **a / some** onions, please?
2. May I have **a / some** lemon, please?
3. May I have **a / some** pears, please?
4. May I have **an / some** orange, please?
5. May I have **a / some** carrots, please?

Now listen and repeat.

17.9 Read the questions and check off the correct pictures.

May I have some tomatoes, please?

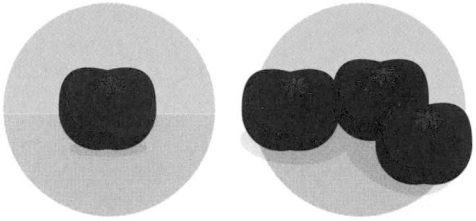

A ☐ B ☑

1 May I have a potato, please?

A ☐ B ☐

2 May I have some coconuts, please?

A ☐ B ☐

3 May I have an apple, please?

A ☐ B ☐

4 May I have a kiwi, please?

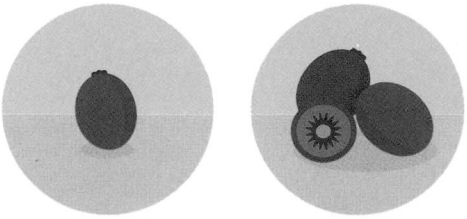

A ☐ B ☐

5 May I have some bananas, please?

A ☐ B ☐

Now listen and repeat.

18 At the toy store

18.1 Listen and write the correct words in the spaces.

ball
action figure
~~alien~~
teddy bear
monster
doll
puppet
car
board game
train
rocket
video game
the moon
balloons
stars
robot

TOYS
9 r
10 t
11 s
12 r
13 b
14 t
15 v
16 b
It's Ben's birthday.
Let's give him a robot.
TOYS

18.2 Listen and check off the correct pictures.

A ☐

B ☑

1

A ☐

B ☐

2

A ☐

B ☐

3

A ☐

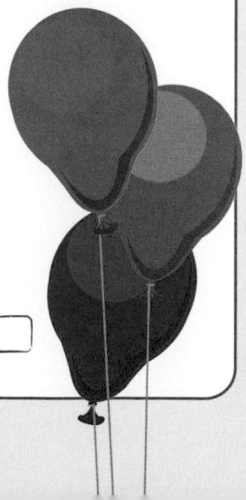

B ☐

18.3 Look at the pictures and write the letters in the correct order.

a i n l e

a l i e n

1

d l o l

d ___ ___ ___

2

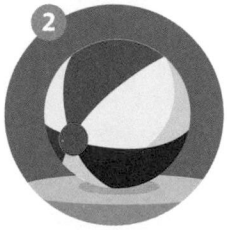

b l l a

b ___ ___ ___

3

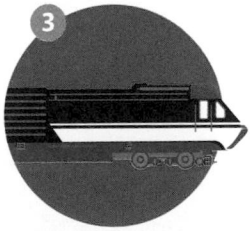

t n r a i

t ___ ___ ___ ___

4

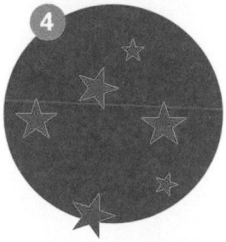

s r t s a

s ___ ___ ___ ___

Now listen and repeat.

18.4 Look at the pictures and circle the correct words.

(doll) / ball

1

car / teddy bear

2

the moon / train

3

board game / monster

4

alien / puppet

Now listen and repeat.

18.5 Look at the pictures and write the correct words in the spaces.

monster ~~stars~~ robot car

stars

1

_____

2

_____

3

_____

Now listen and repeat.

18.6 Listen and write the correct answers in the spaces.

No, she doesn't. ~~Yes, he does.~~
Yes, she does. No, he doesn't.

Does he like aliens?

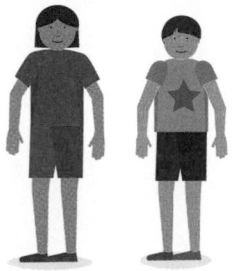

Yes, he does.

1 Does she like board games?

_____

2 Does she like video games?

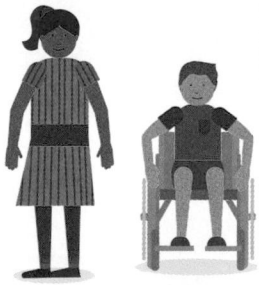

_____.

3 Does he like robots?

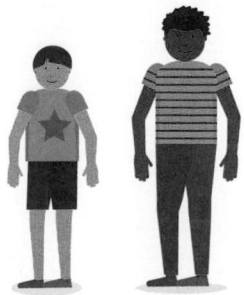

_____

18.7 Look at the pictures and circle the correct words.

Ben likes / doesn't like trains.

1 She **likes / doesn't like** puppets.

2 Maria **likes / doesn't like** aliens.

3 He **likes / doesn't like** cars.

4 Sara **likes / doesn't like** rockets.

5 Max **likes / doesn't like** monsters.

6 He **likes / doesn't like** dolls.

7 She **likes / doesn't like** balloons.

Now listen and repeat.

18.8 Listen and check off the correct answers.

I love cars!

Me too! ☑

I don't. ☐

1. I love teddy bears!

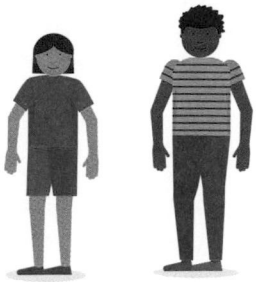

Me too! ☐

I don't. ☐

2. I love video games!

Me too! ☐

I don't. ☐

3. I love action figures!

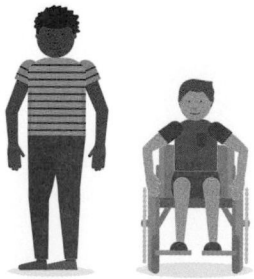

Me too! ☐

I don't. ☐

18.9 Listen to the song and write the correct words in the spaces.
18.10 Color in the three toys that you heard in the song.

Maria likes dolls ,
but she doesn't like _____ .
Andy likes _____ ,
but he doesn't like _____ .
I like _____ and video games,
and my favorite toy
is my _____ !

19 Our hobbies

19.1 Listen and write the correct words in the spaces.

① ride a bike

② w

draw pictures

~~ride a bike~~

paint

skateboard

watch soccer

play the guitar

read

take photos

play the piano

dance

sing

③ s

④ d

I enjoy painting.

Me too. It's fun!

⑤ p

6 r
7 s
8 d
9 p
10 p
11 t

19.2 Read the words and check off the correct pictures.

play the guitar

A ☑ B ☐

1 read

A ☐ B ☐

2 draw pictures

A ☐ B ☐

3 dance

A ☐ B ☐

4 take photos

A ☐ B ☐

5 skateboard

A ☐ B ☐

Now listen and repeat.

19.3 Look at the pictures and circle the correct words.

read / ride a bike

1 dance / skateboard

2 play the piano / read

3 sing / paint

4 watch soccer / sing

Now listen and repeat.

19.4 Match the pictures to the correct words.

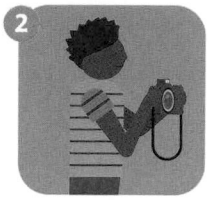

ride a bike play the piano draw pictures take photos play the guitar

Now listen and repeat.

19.5 Look at the pictures and write the letters in the correct order.

d n e c a p n t a i r d e a

d a n c e 1 p ___ ___ ___ 2 r ___ ___

s g n i

3 s ___ ___

Now listen and repeat.

19.6 Match the pictures to the correct sentences.

I like playing the guitar.

1 

I like playing the piano.

2 

I enjoy skateboarding.

3 

I like taking photos.

4 

I like drawing pictures.

5 

I enjoy riding a bike.

Now listen and repeat.

19.7 Listen and check off the correct sentences.

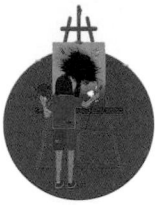

I like painting. ☑
I don't like painting. ☐

1 

I like reading. ☐
I don't like reading. ☐

2 

I like singing. ☐
I don't like singing. ☐

3 

I like painting. ☐
I don't like painting. ☐

4 

I like dancing. ☐
I don't like dancing. ☐

19.8 Look at the pictures and write the correct words in the spaces.

drawing pictures ~~painting~~ reading
taking photos riding a bike

I enjoy painting.

1 

I like _____.

2 

I like _____.

3 

I enjoy _____.

4 

I like _____.

Now listen and repeat.

19.9 There are four sentences . Mark the beginning and end of each one and write them below.

Do you like reading?

1 _____

2 _____

3 _____

Doyoulikereading?|Yes,Ido.Doyoulikesinging?No,Idon't.

Now listen and repeat.

19.10 Look at the pictures and write the correct words in the spaces.

I don't ~~Do you like~~ reading
I do Do you like No

Do you like skateboarding?
Yes, I do.

1 Do you like watching soccer?
Yes, _____ .

2 Do you like dancing?
No, _____ .

3 _____ playing the piano?
Yes, I do.

4 Do you like singing?
_____ , I don't .

5 Do you like _____ ?
Yes, I do.

Now listen and repeat.

19.11 Listen and write the correct answers in the spaces.

~~Yes, I do.~~ No, I don't.
Yes, I do. No, I don't.
Yes, I do.

Do you like reading?

Yes, I do.

1 Do you like riding a bike?

2 Do you like playing the guitar?

3 Do you like singing?

4 Do you like painting?

19.12 Listen to the song and write the correct words in the spaces.

Do you have hobbies?
Yes, I do.
I love reading books
and skateboarding, too.

Do you like playing _____ ?
Yes, I do.
I love _____ tennis
and playing _____ , too.

Do you _____ singing?
Yes, I do.
I love _____ songs,
and I love _____ , too.

20 Review: What I like

20.1 Listen and read.

I'm Andy. I enjoy playing tennis. I like oranges and pears, but I don't like tomatoes. I love video games.

My friend Eva enjoys playing table tennis. She likes watermelons, but she doesn't like pears. My friend loves robots.

20.2 Write about the things you and a friend like then draw a picture.

I'm _____. I enjoy _____.
I like _____ and _____,
but I don't like _____.
I love _____.

My friend _____ enjoys _____.
_____ likes _____, but
_____ doesn't like _____.
My friend loves _____.

21 Our party clothes

21.1 Listen and write the correct words in the spaces.

1 watch

2 s

3 s

4 s

5 p

6 T-

7 h

8 d

9 p

pants sock watch shorts
T-shirt purse hat skirt dress
jeans baseball cap glasses shoe
jacket shirt bag boot
10 b
11 j
12 s
13 b
14 g
15 s
16 b
17 j

21.2 Look at the pictures and circle the correct words.

shirt / (shorts)

1. glasses / boot

2. T-shirt / hat

3. jacket / shoe

4. pants / skirt

5. purse / jeans

Now listen and repeat.

21.3 Look at the pictures and write the correct words in the spaces.

shirt ~~hat~~ jeans dress
watch shorts jacket

It's a hat.

1. It's a _____.

2. It's a _____.

3. They're _____.

4. It's a _____.

5. It's a _____.

6. They're _____.

Now listen and repeat.

21.4 Listen and check off the correct pictures.

A ☐ B ☑

1 A ☐ B ☐

2 A ☐ B ☐

3 A ☐ B ☐

4 A ☐ B ☐

5 A ☐ B ☐

21.5 Listen to the song and write the correct words in the spaces.

We're at a ___party___ ,
so let's all _____ and play.
What a fun _____
for Ben's birthday!

Andy's _____ his
favorite _____ ,
and Sara has
a beautiful _____ .

21.6 Look at the pictures and check off the correct sentences.

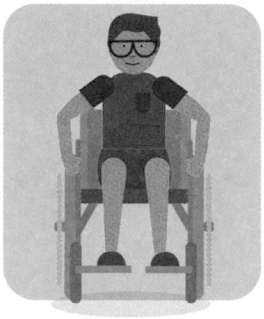

I'm wearing socks. ☐
I'm wearing glasses. ☑

1

I'm wearing a jacket. ☐
I'm wearing pants. ☐

2

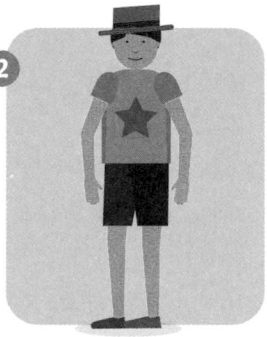

I'm wearing a hat. ☐
I'm wearing a watch. ☐

3

I'm wearing a watch. ☐
I'm wearing jeans. ☐

4

I'm wearing a dress. ☐
I'm wearing boots. ☐

5

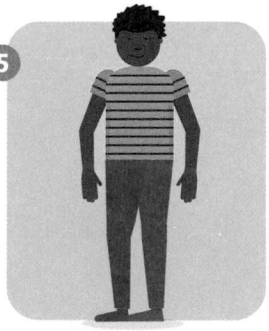

I'm wearing pants. ☐
I'm wearing a hat. ☐

Now listen and repeat.

21.7 Listen and match the names to the correct clothes.

Sara ❶ Max ❷ Nick ❸ Kim ❹ James ❺ Maria

jacket

shorts

dress

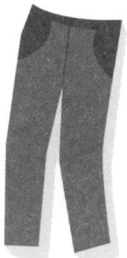

jeans

baseball cap

shirt

21.8 There are four sentences. Mark the beginning and end of each one and write them below.

Areyouwearingboots?|Yes,Iam.Areyouwearingawatch?No,I'mnot.

Are you wearing boots?

❶ _____

❷ _____

❸ _____

Now listen and repeat.

21.9 Look at the pictures and write the correct answers in the spaces.

No, I'm not. ~~Yes, I am.~~ No, I'm not. Yes, I am.

Are you wearing my baseball cap?

Yes, I am.

1. Are you wearing my pants?

_____

2. Are you wearing my shirt?

_____

3. Are you wearing my boots?

_____

Now listen and repeat.

21.10 Look at the pictures and circle the correct words.

What a / What
lovely watch!

1 What a / What
clean shoes!

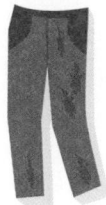

2 What a / What
dirty jeans!

3 What a / What
nice hat!

4 What a / What
colorful bag!

5 What a / What
nice skirt!

Now listen and repeat.

21.11 Match the pictures to the correct sentences.

1 

2 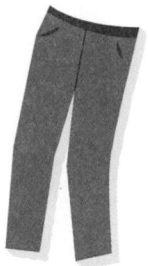

3 

4 

What lovely pants!

What a nice watch!

What dirty socks!

What a beautiful dress!

What lovely shorts!

Now listen and repeat.

22 Our day at the beach

22.1 Listen and write the correct words in the spaces.

jellyfish
play soccer
surf
~~seagull~~
ship
drink juice
eat ice cream
fly a kite
bucket
listen to music
sand
shovel
run on the beach
swim in the ocean
fish
throw a ball
shell
read a book

22.2 Match the pictures to the correct words.

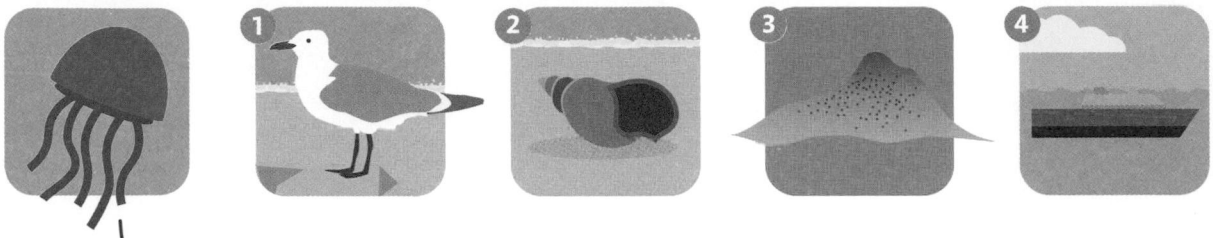

shell sand jellyfish ship seagull

Now listen and repeat.

22.3 Listen and color in the pictures.

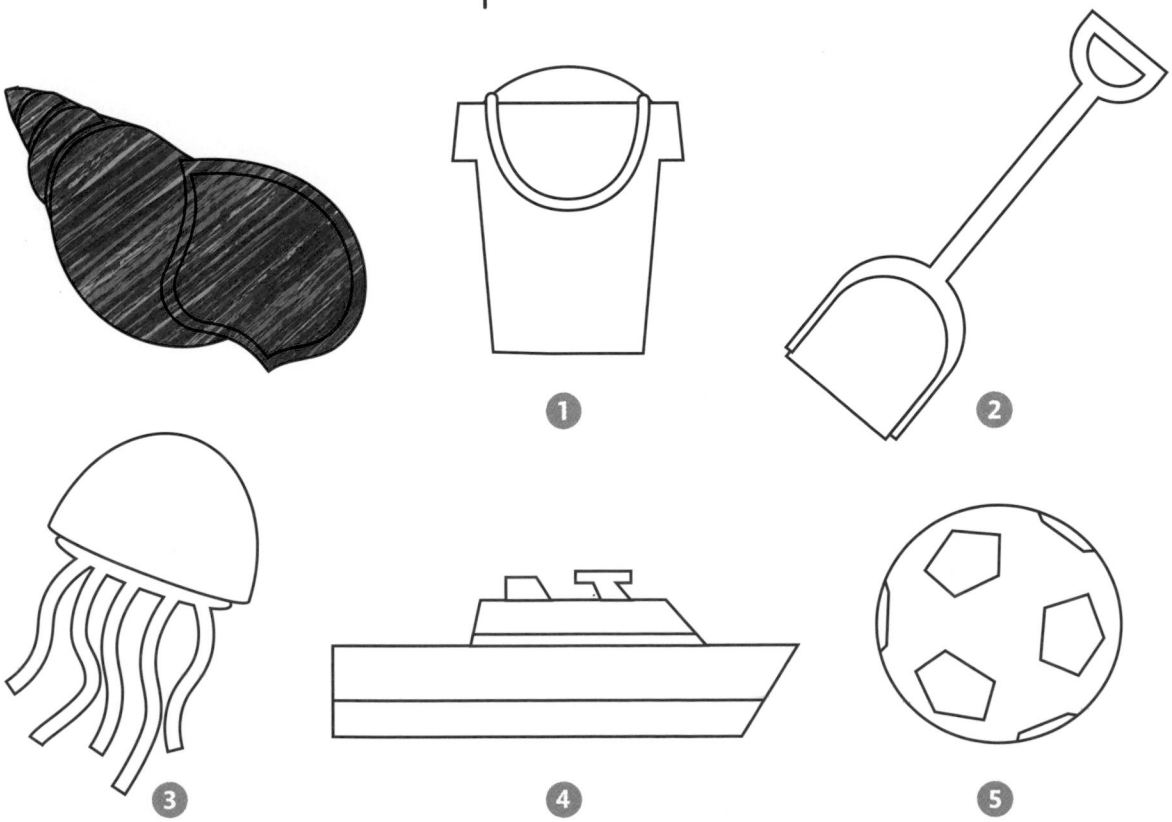

22.4 Read the sentences and check off the correct pictures.

I'm listening to music.

A ☑

B ☐

1 I'm fishing.

A ☐

B ☐

2 I'm playing soccer.

A ☐

B ☐

3 I'm reading a book.

A ☐

B ☐

4 I'm throwing a ball.

A ☐

B ☐

5 I'm running on the beach.

A ☐

B ☐

6 I'm surfing.

A ☐

B ☐

7 I'm swimming in the ocean.

A ☐

B ☐

Now listen and repeat.

22.5 Look at the pictures and circle the correct words.

She's / She isn't reading a book.

1 He's / He isn't swimming.

2 He's / He isn't listening to music.

3 She's / She isn't drinking juice.

4 She's / She isn't surfing.

5 He's / He isn't flying a kite.

6 She's / She isn't running.

Now listen and repeat.

22.6 Look at the pictures and write the correct words in the spaces.

surfing ~~throwing~~ playing listening drinking reading

He's throwing a ball.

1 She's _____ juice.

2 She's _____ .

3 He's _____ soccer.

4 She's _____ a book.

5 He's _____ to music.

Now listen and repeat.

22.7 Look at the pictures and check off the correct answers.

Is Peter fishing?

- Yes, he is. ☑
- No, he isn't. ☐

1. Is he reading a book?

- Yes, he is. ☐
- No, he isn't. ☐

2. Is he flying a kite?

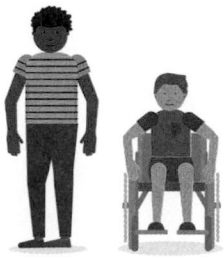

- Yes, he is. ☐
- No, he isn't. ☐

3. Is she playing soccer?

- Yes, she is. ☐
- No, she isn't. ☐

4. Is Maria eating ice cream?

- Yes, she is. ☐
- No, she isn't. ☐

Now listen and repeat.

22.8 Listen and write the correct answers in the spaces.

Yes, she is. ~~Yes, he is.~~
No, he isn't. No, she isn't.

Is he playing soccer?

Yes, he is.

1 Is he flying a kite?

_____

2 Is she reading a book?

_____

3 Is she surfing?

_____

23 Lunchtime

23.1 Listen and write the correct words in the spaces.

1. pie
2. c
3. f
4. c
5. b
6. o
7. s
8. r
9. s

burger salad orange ~~pie~~
fries rice cake candy
sausages drinks chocolate juice
noodles lemonade water fruit
10 c
11 n
12 d
13 f
14 j
15 w
16 l

23.2 Match the pictures to the correct words.

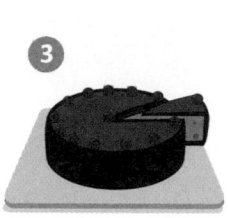

cake candy pie drinks fruit

Now listen and repeat.

23.3 Look at the pictures and write the words in the correct place on the crossword.

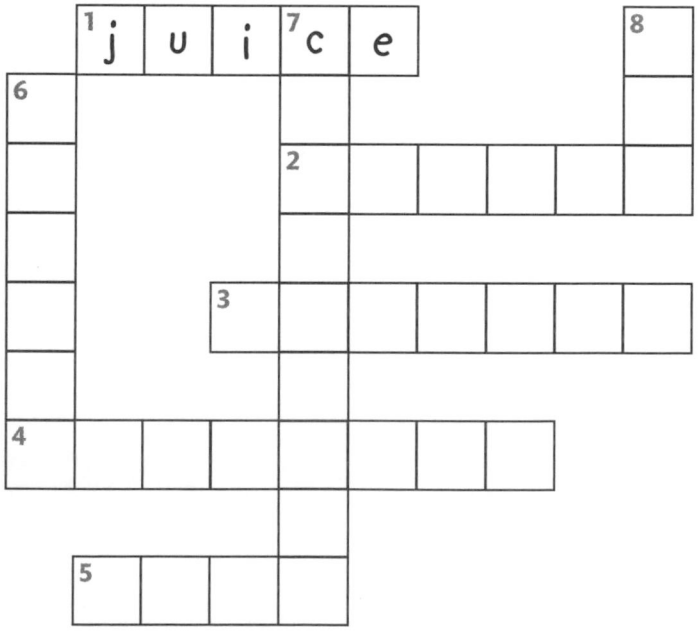

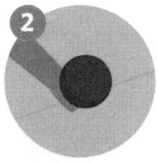

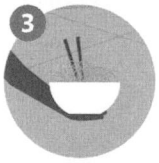

23.4 Listen and match the questions to the correct answers.

What would you like?

1 What would you like?

2 What would you like?

3 What would you like?

4 What would you like?

I'd like some fries, please.

I'd like some water, please.

I'd like an orange, please.

I'd like a burger, please.

I'd like some lemonade, please.

23.5 Look at the pictures and circle the correct words.

I'd like **a** / **some** fruit, please.

1 I'd like **a** / **some** juice, please.

2 I'd like **a** / **some** rice, please.

3 I'd like **an** / **some** orange, please.

4 I'd like **a** / **some** burger, please.

5 I'd like **a** / **some** noodles, please.

Now listen and repeat.

23.6 Listen and write the correct words in the spaces.

No, I wouldn't. No, thank you. ~~Yes, I would.~~
Yes, please. Yes, I would.

Would you like some chocolate?

Yes, I would.

1 

Would you like a drink?

_____

2 

Would you like some salad?

_____

3 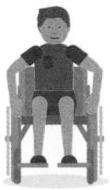

Would you like some fries?

_____

4 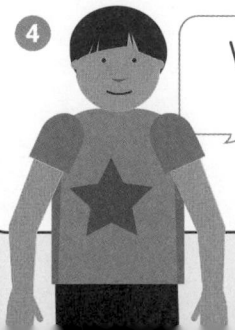

Would you like some cake?

_____

23.7 Listen and write the correct words in the spaces.

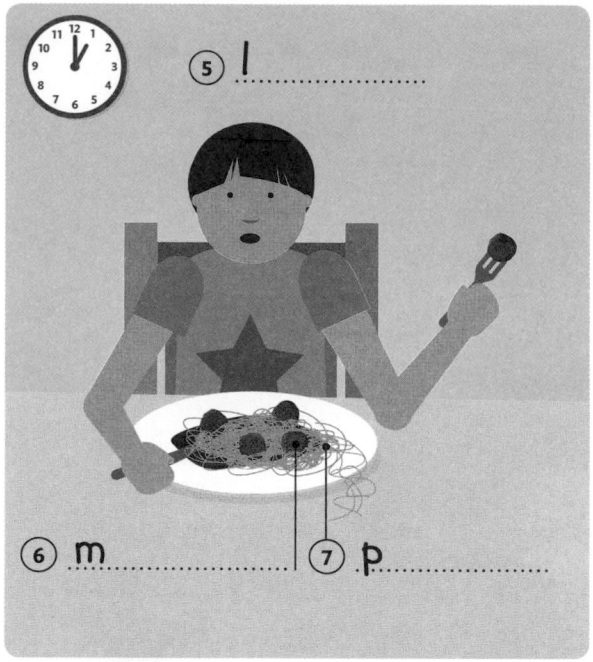

egg	lunch	potatoes	~~breakfast~~	bread
pasta	rice	meatball		chicken
beans	fish	milk	dinner	peas

23.8 Listen and match the questions to the correct answers.

What's for breakfast today, Mom?	Meat and potatoes.
1 What's for lunch today, Dad?	Chicken and peas.
2 What's for breakfast today, Dad?	Fish and beans.
3 What's for dinner today, Mom?	Eggs and bread.
4 What's for lunch today, Mom?	Meatballs and rice.
5 What's for dinner today, Dad?	Milk and bread.

23.9 There are four sentences. Mark the beginning and end of each one and write them below.

What'sforlunch?/Fishandpotatoes.What'sfordinner?pastaandmeatballs.

What's for lunch?

1 _____

2 _____

3 _____

Now listen and repeat.

24 At the park

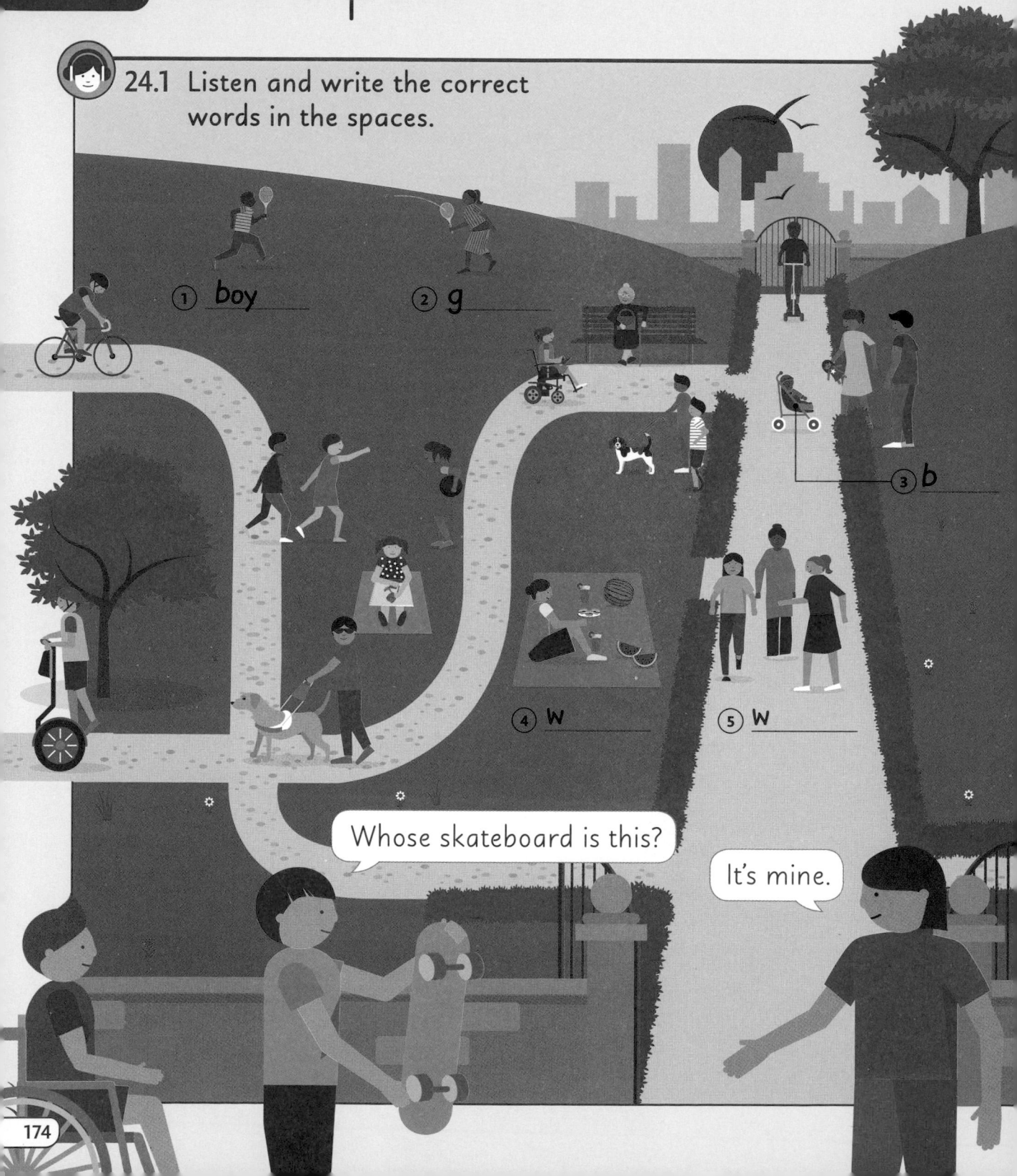

baby woman girl ~~boy~~
women child/kid person men
children/kids man people
6 p
7 p
8 c
9 c
10 m
11 m

24.2 Listen and check off the correct pictures.

A ☐

B ☑

1 A ☐

B ☐

2 A ☐

B ☐

3 A ☐

B ☐

24.3 Look at the pictures and write the correct words in the spaces.

girl men ~~baby~~
boy children woman

baby

1 _____

2 _____

3 _____

4 _____

5 _____

Now listen and repeat.

24.4 Match the pictures to the correct words.

kids boy girl man baby

Now listen and repeat.

24.5 Read the words and check off the correct pictures.

men

A ☐ B ☑

1 person

A ☐ B ☐

2 children

A ☐ B ☐

3 man

A ☐ B ☐

4 kid

A ☐ B ☐

5 women

A ☐ B ☐

Now listen and repeat.

24.6 Rewrite the questions in the correct order.

bike? | Is | Tom's | this

Is this Tom's bike?

1. Kim's | Is | this | ball?

2. this | Nick's | cat? | Is

3. book? | this | Is | Amy's

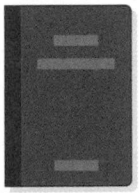

4. Lucy's | Is | this | computer?

5. this | Maria's | jacket? | Is

Now listen and repeat.

24.7 Listen and write the correct names in the spaces.
24.8 Listen again and color in the pictures.

Kim Sam ~~Sara~~
Ann Andy Matt

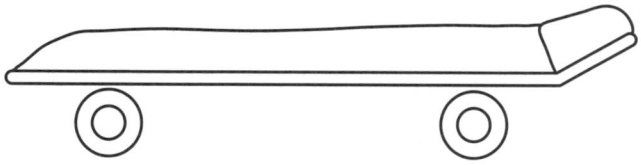

Sara _____

1 _____

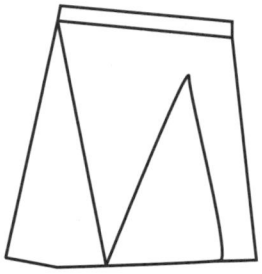

2 _____

3 _____

4 _____

5 _____

24.9 Listen and check off the correct answers.

Whose doll is this?

- It's hers. ☑
- It's yours. ☐

1. Whose watch is this?

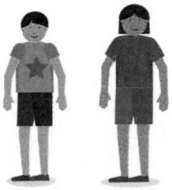

- It's mine. ☐
- It's his. ☐

2. Whose ruler is this?

- It's ours. ☐
- It's theirs. ☐

3. Whose apple is this?

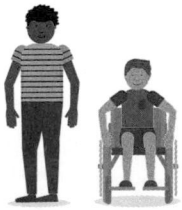

- It's yours. ☐
- It's hers. ☐

4. Whose rabbit is this?

- It's mine. ☐
- It's theirs. ☐

24.10 Listen and circle the correct words.

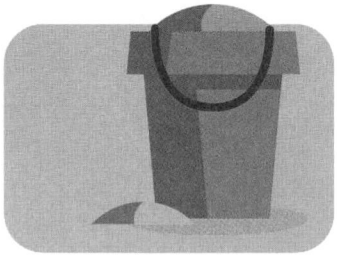

Whose bucket is this?

It's mine / theirs.

1 Whose camera is this?

It's his / hers.

2 Whose tortoise is this?

It's ours / theirs.

3 Whose purse is this?

It's hers / mine.

4 Whose juice is this?

It's yours / his.

5 Whose bike is this?

It's mine / theirs.

6 Whose skateboard is this?

It's hers / ours.

7 Whose ball is this?

It's ours / yours.

25 My day

25.1 Listen and write the correct sentences in the spaces.

① I get up.

⑫ I g

I eat dinner. I call my friend.

I go swimming.

~~I get up.~~ I go to sleep.

⑪ I e

⑩ I g

⑨ I c

② I m
③ I e
④ I b
I go home.
I make my bed.
I walk to school.
I eat breakfast.
I brush my teeth.
I eat lunch.
I study English.
⑤ I w
⑧ I g
⑦ I e
⑥ I s

25.2 Look at the pictures and check off the correct sentences.

I walk to school. ☐
I eat breakfast. ☑

1

I go home. ☐
I call my friend. ☐

2

I get up. ☐
I make my bed. ☐

3

I brush my teeth. ☐
I eat dinner. ☐

4

I go swimming. ☐
I walk to school. ☐

5

I go to sleep. ☐
I study English. ☐

Now listen and repeat.

25.3 Rewrite the sentences in the correct order.

bed. | my | make | I

I make my bed.

1. call | my | I | friend.

2. to | walk | school. | I

3. sleep. | go | I | to

4. my | brush | teeth. | I

5. eat | I | lunch.

Now listen and repeat.

25.4 Look at the clocks and write the correct answers in the spaces.

It's five o'clock. It's six o'clock. ~~It's two o'clock.~~
It's nine o'clock. It's ten o'clock. It's three o'clock.
It's eleven o'clock. It's four o'clock. It's one o'clock.

What time is it?

It's two o'clock.

1 What time is it?

2 What time is it?

3 What time is it?

4 What time is it?

5 What time is it?

6 What time is it?

7 What time is it?

8 What time is it?

Now listen and repeat.

25.5 Match the pictures to the correct words.

In the afternoon

At night

In the morning

In the evening

Now listen and repeat.

25.6 Listen and circle the correct words.

I go swimming in the
morning / afternoon.

I walk to school in the
morning / evening.

I eat dinner in the
afternoon / evening.

I go home in the
morning / afternoon.

I go to sleep at
night / afternoon.

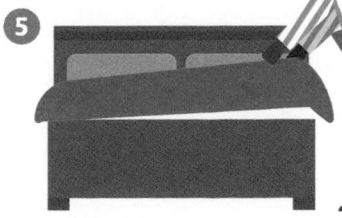

I make my bed in the
evening / morning.

25.7 Read the sentences and write the correct words in the spaces.

in ~~eight o'clock~~ morning When do you at four o'clock

When do you walk to school?

I walk to school at eight o'clock.

1 _____ get up?

I get up at seven o'clock.

2 When do you eat dinner?

I eat dinner _____ the evening.

3 When do you go to sleep?

I go to sleep _____ eight o'clock.

4 When do you go home?

I go home at _____.

5 When do you brush your teeth?

I brush my teeth in the _____ and at night.

Now listen and repeat.

25.8 Look at the pictures and check off the correct sentences.

He goes to sleep. ☑
He go to sleep. ☐

We walks to school. ☐
We walk to school. ☐

She calls her friend. ☐
She calls her friend. ☐

He brushes his teeth. ☐
He brush his teeth. ☐

They eats dinner. ☐
They eat dinner. ☐

I goes home. ☐
I go home. ☐

Now listen and repeat.

25.9 Write the letters in the correct order.

M d n o a y

M o n d a y

1 T s d u y e a

T _ _ _ _ _ _

2 W d n e a s e y d

W _ _ _ _ _ _ _ _ _

3 T u r a s y h d

T _ _ _ _ _ _ _ _

4 F i d y r a

F _ _ _ _ _ _

5 S u t a d y a r

S _ _ _ _ _ _ _ _

6 S d n a y u

S _ _ _ _ _ _

Now listen and repeat.

25.10 Read the sentences and circle the correct words.

I walk to school (at) / on seven o'clock.

1 I go swimming at / on Tuesdays.

2 I call my friend at / on Fridays.

3 I eat lunch at / on twelve o'clock.

Now listen and repeat.

25.11 Listen and write the correct answers in the spaces.

I don't. ~~So do I.~~ I don't. So do I.

I eat breakfast at seven o'clock.

So do I.

1 I make my bed in the morning.

2 I study English on Wednesdays.

3 I go home at four o'clock.

26 Review: Me and my day

26.1 Listen and read.

My name's Maria. Today I'm wearing a dress and shoes. My favorite food is cake and I love burgers, too.

I get up at 7 o'clock and I eat breakfast.
In the evening, I call my friend.
I study English on Tuesdays.
On Saturdays, I go swimming.

26.2 Write about the things you do then draw a picture of your favorite foods.

My name's _____. Today I'm wearing _____ and _____. My favorite food is _____ and I love _____, too.

I get up at _____ and I _____.
In the evening, I _____.
I study English on _____.
On Saturdays, I _____.

Handwriting guide

A1 To practice writing English letters, start at the red dot and then follow the arrows.

A a

B b

C c

D d

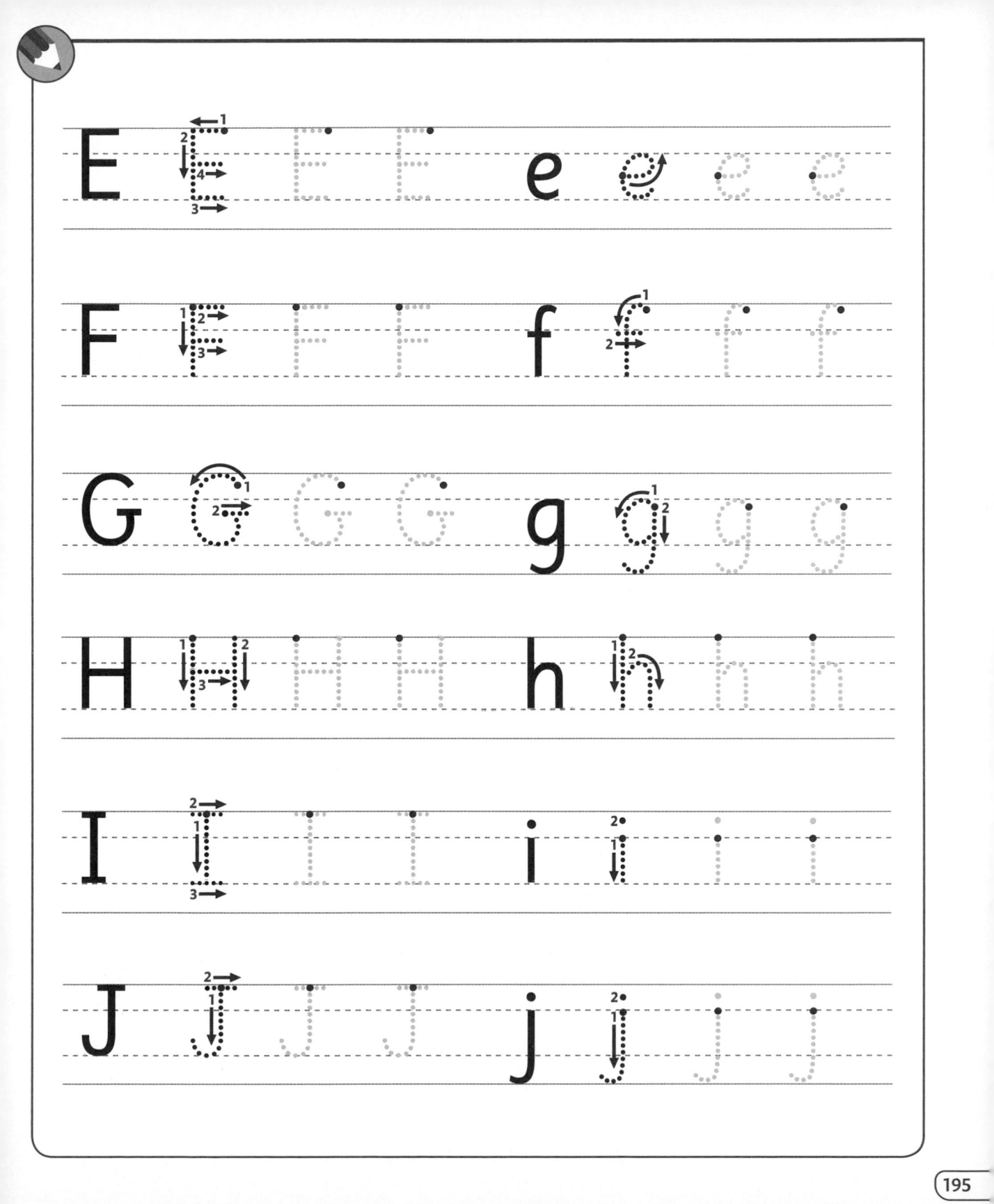
E
e
F
f
G
g
H
h
I
i
J
j

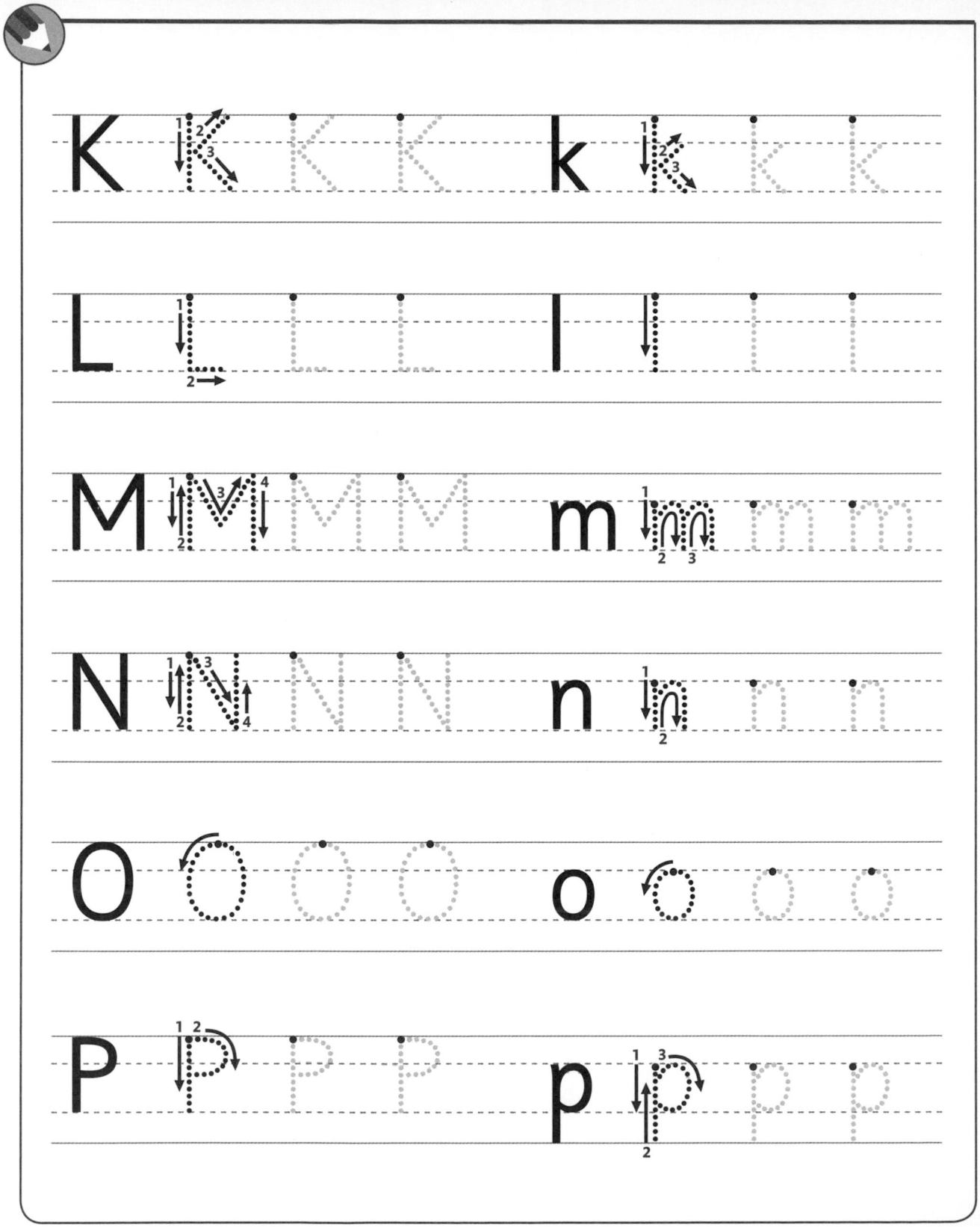
K k
L l
M m
N n
O o
P p

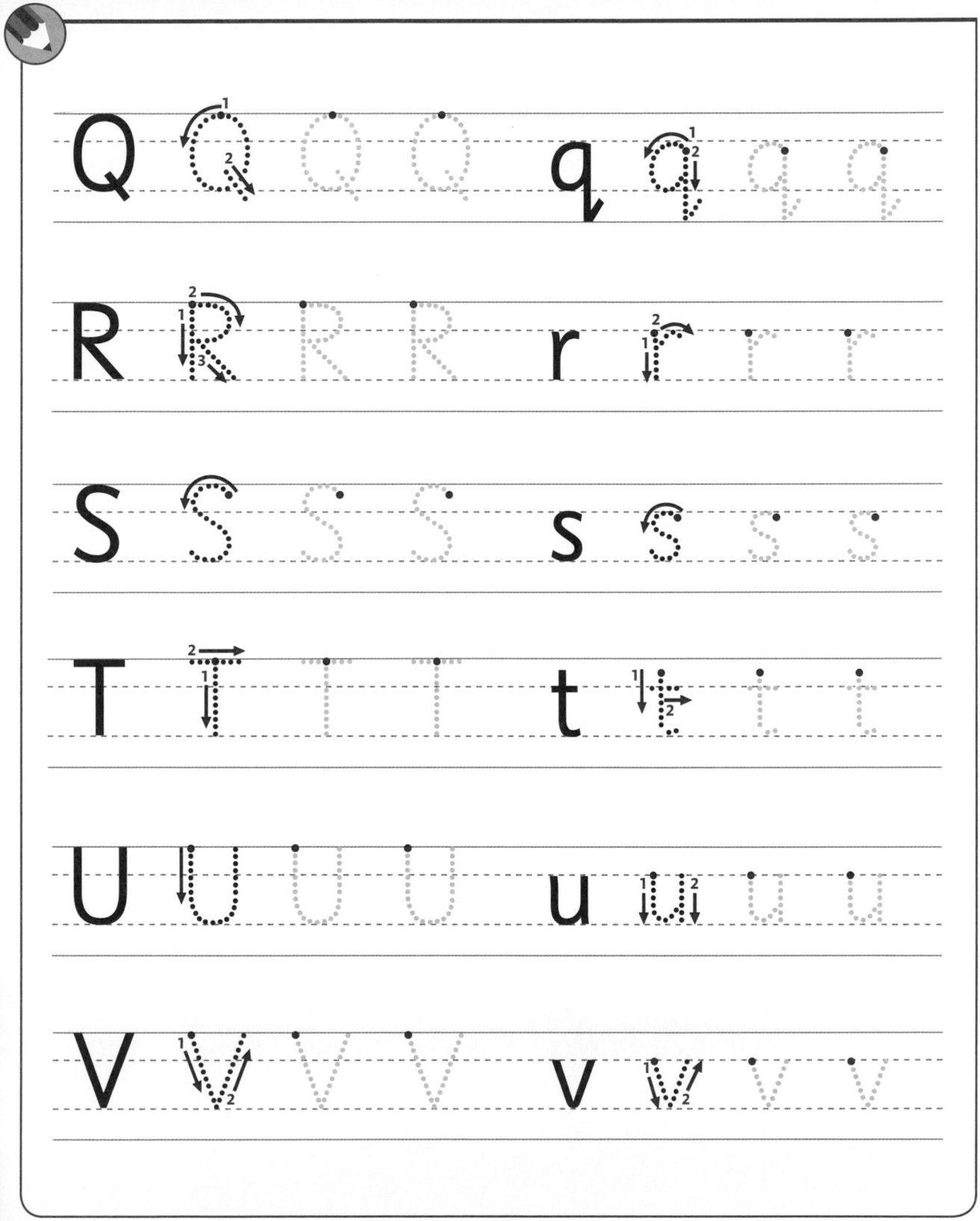
Q q
R r
S s
T t
U u
V v

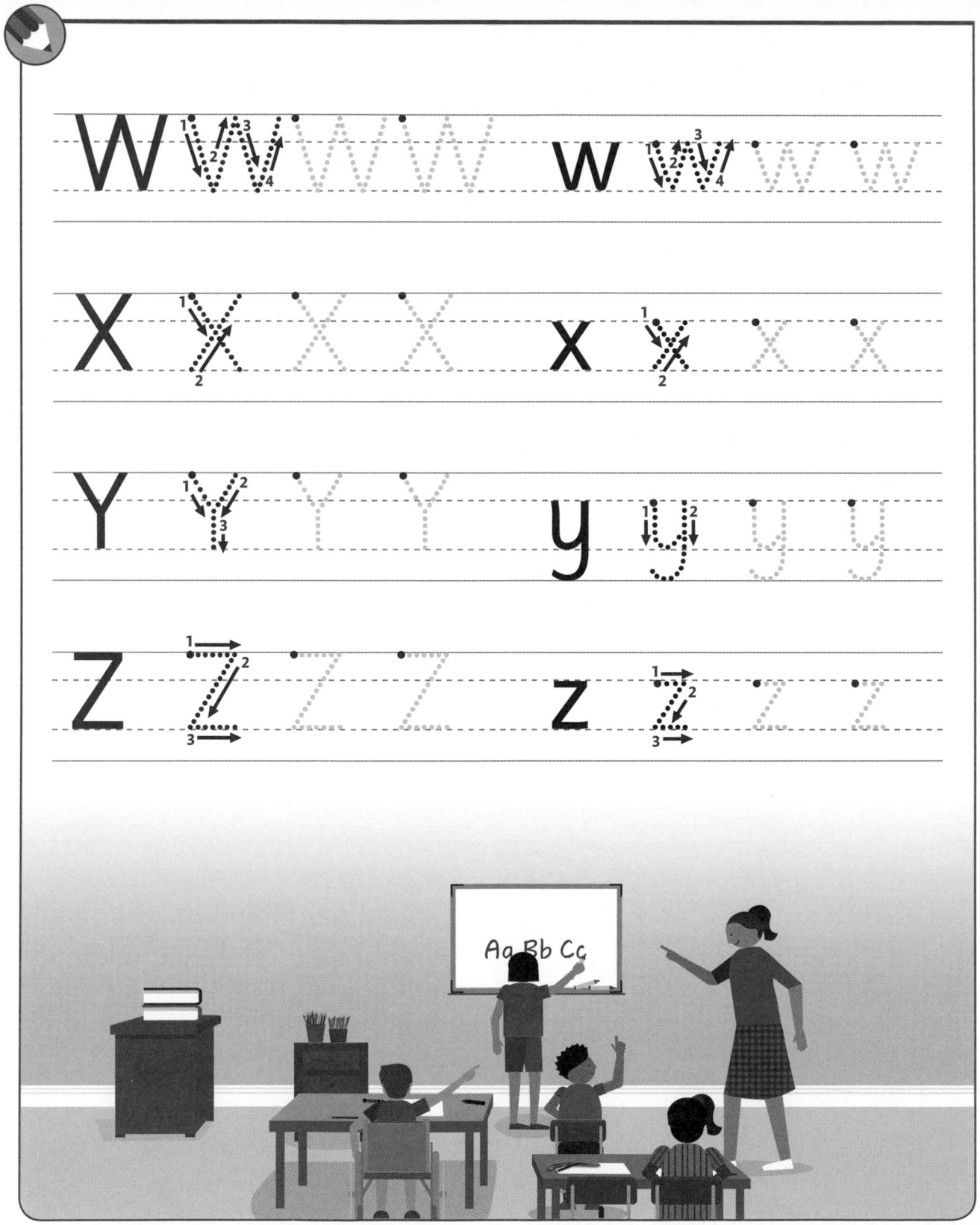
Aa Bb Cc

Answers

1

1.1

1. Maria
2. Ben
3. Max
4. Andy
5. Sofia
6. Sara

1.2

1. Hi, my **name's** Sara.
2. Hi, I'm **Max**.
3. Hi, **I'm** Andy.
4. Hello, I'm **Maria**.
5. **Hello**, I'm Ben.

1.3

1.4

1. Andy
2. Sara
3. Max
4. Maria
5. Sofia

1.5

1. three
2. seven
3. nine
4. six
5. ten
6. eight
7. five

1.6

1. eight
2. two
3. four
4. one
5. seven

1.7

1. one
2. two
3. five
4. four
5. six

1.8

1. I'm fine, thanks.
2. I'm nine years old.

2

2.1

1. playground
2. numbers
3. letters
4. teacher
5. board
6. classmate
7. alphabet
8. tablet
9. cupboard
10. book

2.2

1. tablet
2. teacher
3. alphabet
4. board

5 playground 6 letters
7 numbers 8 classmate
9 cupboard

2.3

1 cupboard 2 numbers
3 tablet 4 teacher
5 board 6 book

2.4

1 A 2 B 3 A 4 A 5 B

2.5

1 pick up 2 sit down
3 find 4 stand up
5 ask

2.6

1 show 2 listen 3 close
4 find 5 answer

2.7

1 find 2 ask 3 show
4 look 5 open 6 close
7 add 8 answer

2.8

1 **His** name's Andy.
2 **His** name's Ben.
3 **Her** name's Maria.
4 **His** name's Max.
5 **Her** name's Sofia.

2.9

1 His name's Dan.
2 Her name's Bella.
3 His name's Tom.
4 Her name's Anna.
5 Her name's Amy.

2.10

1 Her name's Evie.
2 What's his name?
3 His name's Jack.

3

3.1

1 write 2 read 3 count
4 play 5 spell 6 paint
7 draw

3.2

1 read 2 play 3 write
4 paint

3.3

1 A 2 A 3 B 4 A 5 A

3.4

1. Let's write!
2. Let's count!
3. Let's paint!
4. Let's read!
5. Let's play!

3.5

Hello, **hello**!
What's your **name**?
How are you?
Let's **play** a game.

Let's say hello
to my new friends
Max and Maria,
Sara and **Ben**.

3.6

1. twelve
2. sixteen
3. fifteen
4. twenty

3.7

1. fourteen
2. nineteen
3. eighteen
4. eleven
5. sixteen
6. twenty
7. thirteen
8. fifteen

3.8

1. tablet
2. numbers
3. cars
4. dog
5. cupboard

3.9

1. A
2. B
3. B
4. B

4

4.1

1. pink
2. book
3. crayon
4. eraser
5. pen
6. paper
7. ball
8. notepad
9. purple
10. red
11. book pack
12. ruler
13. white
14. brown
15. apple
16. orange
17. green
18. yellow
19. blue
20. pencil
21. gray
22. black
23. watch

4.2

1. crayon
2. eraser
3. pen
4. pencil
5. watch

4.3

1. green
2. pink
3. brown
4. black
5. gray

4.4

1. purple
2. book pack
3. white
4. notepad
5. orange
6. yellow
7. paper

4.5

1. A
2. A
3. A
4. B
5. B

4.6

1. It's a watch.
2. It's a ball.
3. They're rulers.

4.7

1. What are **these**?
2. It's an **apple**.
3. **It's** a pencil.
4. **What are** these?
5. **They're** notepads.

4.8

4.9

1. B
2. A
3. B
4. A

4.10

1. It's purple.
2. It's red.
3. It's orange.

5

5.1

1. zebra
2. giraffe
3. lion
4. elephant
5. hippo
6. parrot
7. tiger
8. monkey

9 bear
10 frog
11 snake
12 polar bear
13 bird
14 whale
15 penguin
16 crocodile
17 lizard

5.2

1 hippo
2 parrot
3 tiger
4 elephant
5 crocodile

5.3

w	s	f	r	o	g
h	g	a	s	l	v
a	b	w	n	z	x
l	i	z	a	r	d
e	r	y	k	c	k
f	d	b	e	a	r

5.4

1 whale
2 lion
3 zebra
4 bear

5.5

Animals, animals
everywhere!
a **lion**, a giraffe,
and a **polar bear**.

A **whale** and
a **penguin**,
a tiger and a **snake**,
animals, animals,
they are great!

5.6

1 What's **that**?
2 **They're** hippos.
3 **What's** that?

5.7

1 It's a zebra.
2 It's a crocodile.
3 They're parrots.

5.8

1 It's a lizard.
2 They're penguins.
3 It's a parrot.
4 They're elephants.
5 It's a bird.

5.9

1 They're tigers.
2 What's that?
3 It's an elephant.

5.10

1 A 2 A 3 B 4 B 5 A

5.11

1 My favorite animal is a **lizard**.
2 My favorite animal is a **bear**.
3 My favorite animal is a **bird**.
4 My favorite animal is an **elephant**.
5 My favorite animal is a **monkey**.

6

6.1

1 my family
2 my grandmother/grandma
3 my grandfather/grandpa
4 my father/dad
5 my mother/mom
6 my brother
7 my sister
8 me
9 my uncle
10 my aunt
11 my cousin

6.2

1 my grandma
2 my cousin
3 my family
4 my uncle
5 my grandpa

6.3

1 brother
2 mother
3 grandfather
4 sister

6.4

1 She's my **cousin**.
2 He's my **uncle**.
3 She's my **sister**.
4 He's my **dad**.
5 She's my **grandma**.

6.5

1 No, he isn't.
2 No, she isn't.
3 Yes, she is.

6.6

1 doctor
2 teacher
3 chef
4 firefighter

6.7

d	o	c	t	o	r	g	f
t	v	y	i	j	w	r	a
t	e	a	c	h	e	r	r
f	t	r	h	y	f	h	m
a	q	g	l	m	b	q	e
w	c	h	e	f	d	m	r

6.8

1. She's a **doctor**.
2. He's a **teacher**.
3. She's a **chef**.
4. She's a **police officer**.

6.9

1. She's a doctor.
2. She's a chef.
3. He's a farmer.
4. She's a teacher.
5. She's a police officer.

6.10

Who's this?
She's my **mother**.
Who's that?
He's my **brother**.

My **dad** is a teacher,
my **mom** is a vet,
Grandpa's a **doctor**,
And Grandma's a **chef**!

7

7.1

1. poster
2. computer
3. mouse
4. keyboard
5. lamp
6. toy box
7. desk
8. doll
9. chair
10. car
11. camera
12. rug
13. bed
14. teddy bear
15. baseball bat
16. ball
17. skateboard
18. tennis racket

7.2

1. skateboard
2. chair
3. toy box
4. car
5. lamp

7.3

1. A
2. B
3. B
4. A

7.4

1. B
2. A
3. B
4. B
5. A

7.5

1. doll
2. skateboard
3. toy box
4. computer

7.6

1. **That's** my ball.
2. **These are** my cameras.
3. **Those are** my teddy bears.
4. **That's** my toy box.
5. **This is** my tennis racket.

7.7

1. Andy
2. Andy
3. Andy
4. Maria
5. Maria
6. Andy
7. Maria

7.8

1. No, I don't.
2. Yes, I do.
3. Yes, I do.
4. No, I don't.

7.9

1. No, I don't.
2. Yes, I do.
3. No, I don't.
4. Yes, I do.
5. No, I don't.

7.10

This is my **toy box**
and these are my **toys**,
I have a **ball**
and a **skateboard**, too.
Toys are fantastic!
Toys are cool!

9

9.1

1. tired
2. hungry
3. thirsty
4. scared
5. hot
6. cold
7. excited
8. sad
9. happy

9.2

1. cold
2. scared
3. hungry
4. sad
5. hot

9.3

1. A
2. A
3. B
4. B
5. A

9.4

1. thirsty
2. tired
3. happy
4. excited

9.5

Are you **happy**?
Yes, we are!
We are at the fair.

Are you **tired**?
No, we aren't.
We aren't tired
or **scared**!

9.6

1. We're happy.
2. We're thirsty.
3. We're really hot.

9.7

1. We're happy.
2. They're cold.
3. They're hot.
4. We're sad.
5. They're thirsty.
6. They're tired.
7. We're scared.

9.8

1. We're really **excited**.
2. They're **hot**.
3. We're **happy**.
4. We're **really** tired.

9.9

1. Yes, we are.
2. Yes, we are.
3. No, they're not.
4. No, we're not.
5. Yes, they are.

9.10

1. Yes, they are.
2. Yes, we are.
3. No, we're not.
4. No, they're not.

9.11

1. No, they're not.
2. No, we're not.
3. Yes, they are.
4. No, they're not.
5. No, we're not.
6. Yes, we are.
7. Yes, they are.

10

10.1

1. rabbit
2. tortoise
3. dog
4. mouse
5. collar
6. spider
7. cat
8. vet
9. fish

10.2

1. old
2. nice
3. scary
4. dirty
5. clean
6. beautiful
7. big
8. small

10.3

1. rabbit
2. fish
3. spider
4. collar

10.4

1. cat
2. vet
3. mouse
4. dog
5. tortoise

10.5

1. A
2. A
3. B
4. B

10.6

I have a **cat**,
she's **black** and **small**.
She likes to run
and play with a ball.

Maria has a **tortoise**,
his name is Socks.
He's **old** and **green**
and he's in this box.

10.7

1. Sara has a tortoise.
2. Ben has a rabbit.
3. She has a fish.
4. She has a cat.
5. He has a cat.

10.8

1. B
2. B
3. B
4. A
5. B

10.9

1. Yes, he does.
2. Yes, she does.
3. No, he doesn't.

10.10

1. A
2. A
3. B
4. A
5. B

10.11

1. The mouse.
2. Which one is scary?
3. The spider!

11

11.1

1. hair
2. nose
3. face
4. long hair
5. mouth
6. body
7. hand
8. arm
9. fingers
10. leg
11. toes
12. foot
13. feet
14. head
15. short hair
16. eye
17. ear
18. teeth

11.2

d	g	f	l	b	x	a
t	e	e	t	h	h	r
r	l	e	g	n	a	m
j	k	t	k	b	i	f
f	i	n	g	e	r	s

11.3

1. long hair
2. ear
3. teeth
4. body

11.4

1. mouth
2. nose
3. head
4. foot
5. hand

11.5

1. A
2. B
3. B

11.6

1. The robot has **purple** eyes.
2. It has red **teeth**.
3. It has purple **legs**.
4. The robot has **blue** feet.
5. It has a **yellow** nose.
6. The robot has orange **hands**.

11.7

11.8

1. Yes, it does.
2. No, it doesn't.
3. No, it doesn't.
4. Yes, it does.
5. No, it doesn't.

11.9

1. No, it doesn't.
2. Yes, it does.
3. No, it doesn't.
4. Yes, it does.
5. Yes, it does.

11.10

1. clap
2. touch
3. move
4. point

11.11

Clap your hands,
touch your nose,
move your feet,
point your toes!

Point one **finger**,
move your head,
wave your arms,
touch one leg!

12

12.1

1. airport
2. airplane
3. street
4. train
5. bike
6. zoo
7. park
8. bookstore
9. lake
10. boat
11. helicopter
12. school
13. fire station
14. apartment block
15. hospital
16. house
17. store
18. truck
19. car
20. bus
21. motorcycle

12.2

1. bus
2. school
3. bike
4. hospital
5. truck

12.3

1. A
2. B
3. A
4. B
5. A

12.4

1. car
2. train
3. lake
4. park

12.5

This is my town,
there's a **park**
and a **zoo**.
There's an **airport**,
a **lake**, and
a fire station, too.

This is my town,
there are **cars** and
a **school**.
This is my town,
I love it, it's cool.

12.6

1. **There are** two stores.
2. **There's** a fire station.
3. **There's** a zoo.
4. **There are** three houses.
5. **There are** four cars.

12.7

1. A
2. B
3. B
4. A
5. A

12.8

1. in front of
2. between
3. next to

12.9

1. It's **behind** the green car.
2. It's **in front of** the lake.
3. It's **next to** the school.
4. It's **between** the hospital and the bookstore.
5. It's **in front of** the hospital.

12.10

1. It's behind the school.
2. It's between the airport and the apartment block.
3. It's next to the lake.
4. It's behind the hospital.
5. It's between the fire station and the store.

13

13.1

1. garden
2. bedroom
3. clock
4. plants
5. wall
6. window
7. floor
8. armchair
9. bookcase
10. bathroom
11. mirror
12. bath
13. living room
14. television/TV
15. couch
16. hall
17. door
18. mat
19. lights
20. kitchen
21. refrigerator
22. dining room
23. flowers
24. table
25. chair

13.2

1. dining room
2. living room
3. kitchen
4. bedroom
5. hall

13.3

1. armchair
2. window
3. table
4. lights

13.4

1. couch
2. door
3. refrigerator

13.5

1. clock
2. bookcase
3. chair
4. plants

13.6

1. on
2. under

13.7

1. The cat is **in** the bath.
2. The plants are **under** the window.
3. The cat is **on** the mat.
4. The bookcase is **under** the lights.
5. The flowers are **on** the table.

13.8

1. A 2. B 3. A 4. A

13.9

The TV's **in**
the living room,
the **mat** is in the **hall**.

Where's the **clock**?
It's **on** my
bedroom **wall**.

13.10

1. No, there isn't.
2. Yes, there is.
3. No, there isn't.
4. Yes, there is.
5. **Is there** a table in the dining room?

13.11

1. No, there aren't.
2. No, there aren't.
3. Yes, there are.
4. Yes, there are.
5. No, there aren't.

15

15.1

1. pig
2. tractor
3. tree
4. sheep
5. barn
6. pond
7. duck
8. chicken
9. cow
10. the sun
11. field
12. goat
13. donkey
14. bee
15. tail
16. horse

15.2

g	t	d	i	h	b
b	a	r	n	o	e
p	i	g	l	r	e
r	l	e	w	s	i
d	o	n	k	e	y

15.3

1. B 2. A 3. B 4. A 5. B

15.4

1. pond
2. tractor
3. the sun
4. tail
5. tree

15.5

1. field
2. barn
3. donkey
4. sheep
5. goat

15.6

1. There are five.
2. There are four.
3. There are three.
4. There are seven.
5. There are six.
6. There are two.

15.7

1. **There are** three.
2. **There's** one.
3. **There are** four.
4. **There's** one.

15.8

1. It's **behind** the tree.
2. It's **next to** the pond.
3. They're **in front of** the barn.

15.9

Where are the **ducks**?
They're in the **pond**!

Where are the **goats**?
They're **in** the field!

Where are the **cows**?
They're in the **barn**!

Where are the animals?
They're **on** my farm!

15.10

1. The ducks are in the pond.
2. The sheep are in front of the barn.
3. The horse is under the tree.

16

16.1

1. basketball
2. baseball
3. soccer
4. tennis
5. badminton
6. swimming
7. table tennis
8. ice hockey

16.2

1. badminton
2. tennis
3. swimming

16.3

1 B 2 A 3 B 4 B 5 B

16.4

1 jump
2 swim
3 play tennis
4 play ice hockey
5 catch
6 bounce
7 kick
8 throw
9 hit

16.5

1 swim
2 kick
3 catch
4 hit

16.6

1 A 2 A 3 B 4 B 5 B

16.7

1 throw
2 jump
3 bounce
4 catch

16.8

1 play badminton
2 play soccer
3 play baseball
4 play basketball
5 play ice hockey

16.9

1 I **can** play tennis.
2 I **can't** play baseball.
3 I **can't** play ice hockey.
4 I **can** play basketball.
5 I **can't** play badminton.
6 I **can** play soccer.

16.10

1 No, I can't.
2 No, I can't.
3 Yes, I can.
4 Yes, I can.

16.11

1 Yes, **he can**.
2 **Can she** run?
3 No, **she can't**.
4 Yes, **she can**.
5 **Can he** play baseball?

16.12

1 Yes, she can.
2 No, she can't.
3 Yes, he can.

16.13

1 Yes, she can.
2 Can he swim?
3 No, he can't.

17

17.1

1. grapes
2. lemons
3. bananas
4. limes
5. kiwis
6. mangoes
7. pineapples
8. tomatoes
9. onions
10. apples
11. pears
12. oranges
13. watermelons
14. coconuts
15. carrots
16. potatoes
17. meat
18. fish
19. fruit
20. vegetables

17.2

1. kiwis
2. pears
3. apples
4. fruit
5. grapes
6. limes
7. meat
8. lemons

17.3

1. watermelons
2. carrots
3. vegetables
4. coconuts

17.4

Apples and oranges,
pears and **mangoes**, too.
Here are nice **potatoes**,
and meat and **fish** for you.

17.5

17.6

1. I like tomatoes **and** carrots.
2. I don't like potatoes **or** onions.
3. I **like** lemons and limes.
4. I don't like apples **or** coconuts.
5. I like mangoes **and** watermelons.

17.7

1. Yes, I do.
2. No, I don't.
3. No, I don't.
4. Yes, I do.

17.8

1. May I have **some** onions, please?
2. May I have **a** lemon, please?
3. May I have **some** pears, please?
4. May I have **an** orange, please?
5. May I have **some** carrots, please?

17.9

1. A 2. B 3. A 4. A 5. B

18

18.1

1. alien
2. puppet
3. teddy bear
4. action figure
5. ball
6. doll
7. monster
8. car
9. rocket
10. the moon
11. stars
12. robot
13. balloons
14. train
15. video game
16. board game

18.2

1. A 2. B 3. B

18.3

1. doll 2. ball 3. train
4. stars

18.4

1. teddy bear
2. the moon
3. board game
4. puppet

18.5

1. monster
2. car
3. robot

18.6

1. No, she doesn't.
2. Yes, she does.
3. No, he doesn't.

18.7

1. She **doesn't like** puppets.
2. Maria **likes** aliens.
3. He **doesn't like** cars.
4. Sara **likes** rockets.
5. Max **likes** monsters.
6. He **doesn't like** dolls.
7. She **likes** balloons.

18.8

1. I don't.
2. Me too!
3. I don't.

18.9

Maria likes **dolls**,
but she doesn't like **puppets**.
Andy likes **cars**,
but he doesn't like **rockets**.
I like **trains** and video games,
and my favorite toy
is my **monster**!

18.10

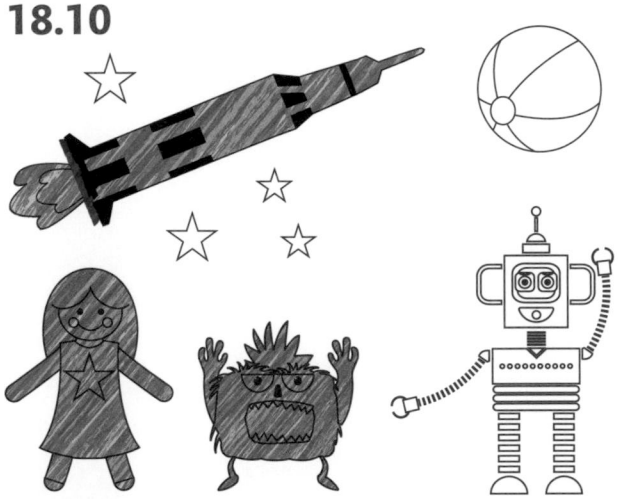

19

19.1

1. ride a bike
2. watch soccer
3. skateboard
4. draw pictures
5. paint
6. read
7. sing
8. dance
9. play the guitar
10. play the piano
11. take photos

19.2

1. B 2. B 3. A 4. A 5. A

19.3

1. skateboard
2. play the piano
3. sing
4. watch soccer

19.4

1. play the guitar
2. take photos
3. ride a bike
4. play the piano

19.5

1. paint 2. read
3. sing

19.6

1. I like taking photos.
2. I like playing the guitar.
3. I enjoy riding a bike.
4. I enjoy skateboarding.
5. I like drawing pictures.

19.7

1. I like reading.
2. I don't like singing.
3. I don't like painting.
4. I like dancing.

19.8

1. I like **drawing pictures**.
2. I like **riding a bike**.
3. I enjoy **taking photos**.
4. I like **reading**.

19.9

1. Yes, I do.
2. Do you like singing?
3. No, I don't.

19.10

1. Yes, **I do**.
2. No, **I don't**.
3. **Do you like** playing the piano?
4. **No**, I don't.
5. Do you like **reading**?

19.11

1. No, I don't.
2. No, I don't.
3. Yes, I do.
4. Yes, I do.

19.12

Do you have hobbies?
Yes, I do.
I **love** reading books
and skateboarding, too.

Do you like playing **tennis**?
Yes, I do.
I love **playing** tennis
and playing **soccer**, too.

Do you **enjoy** singing?
Yes, I do.
I love **singing** songs,
and I love **dancing**, too.

21

21.1

1. watch
2. sock
3. skirt
4. shorts
5. pants
6. T-shirt
7. hat
8. dress
9. purse
10. baseball cap
11. jeans
12. shoe
13. boot
14. glasses
15. shirt
16. bag
17. jacket

21.2

1. glasses
2. T-shirt
3. shoe
4. skirt
5. purse

21.3

1. It's a **watch**.
2. It's a **shirt**.
3. They're **jeans**.
4. It's a **dress**.
5. It's a **jacket**.
6. They're **shorts**.

21.4

1. A
2. B
3. A
4. B
5. A

21.5

We're at a **party**,
so let's all **dance** and play.
What a fun **party**
for Ben's birthday!

Andy's **wearing** his
favorite **T-shirt**,
and Sara has
a beautiful **skirt**.

21.6

1. I'm wearing a jacket.
2. I'm wearing a hat.
3. I'm wearing a watch.
4. I'm wearing boots.
5. I'm wearing pants.

21.7

1. shirt
2. baseball cap
3. jeans
4. shorts
5. dress

21.8

1. Yes, I am.
2. Are you wearing a watch?
3. No, I'm not.

21.9

1. No, I'm not.
2. No, I'm not.
3. Yes, I am.

21.10

1. **What** clean shoes!
2. **What** dirty jeans!
3. **What a** nice hat!
4. **What a** colorful bag!
5. **What a** nice skirt!

21.11

1. What dirty socks!
2. What lovely pants!
3. What lovely shorts!
4. What a beautiful dress!

22

22.1

1. seagull
2. ship
3. surf
4. jellyfish
5. fly a kite
6. sand
7. play soccer
8. bucket
9. shovel
10. listen to music
11. drink juice
12. eat ice cream
13. fish
14. swim in the ocean
15. run on the beach
16. read a book
17. throw a ball
18. shell

22.2

1. seagull
2. shell
3. sand
4. ship

22.3

1. 
2. 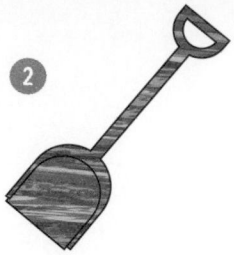
3. 
4. 
5. 

22.4

1. A
2. B
3. B
4. B
5. A
6. B
7. B

22.5

1. **He isn't** swimming.
2. **He's** listening to music.
3. **She isn't** drinking juice.
4. **She isn't** surfing.
5. **He's** flying a kite.
6. **She's** running.

22.6

1. She's **drinking** juice.
2. She's **surfing**.

3. He's **playing** soccer.
4. She's **reading** a book.
5. He's **listening** to music.

22.7

1. No, he isn't.
2. Yes, he is.
3. No, she isn't.
4. Yes, she is.

22.8

1. No, he isn't.
2. No, she isn't.
3. Yes, she is.

23

23.1

1. pie
2. cake
3. fries
4. candy
5. burger
6. orange
7. salad
8. rice
9. sausages
10. chocolate
11. noodles
12. drinks
13. fruit
14. juice
15. water
16. lemonade

23.2

1. fruit
2. drinks
3. cake
4. candy

23.3

1. juice
2. orange
3. noodles
4. sausages
5. rice
6. drinks
7. chocolate
8. pie

23.4

1. I'd like some fries, please.
2. I'd like some lemonade, please.
3. I'd like a burger, please.
4. I'd like some water, please.

23.5

1. I'd like **some** juice, please.
2. I'd like **some** rice, please.
3. I'd like **an** orange, please.
4. I'd like **a** burger, please.
5. I'd like **some** noodles, please.

23.6

1. No, thank you.
2. Yes, please.
3. Yes, I would.
4. No, I wouldn't.

23.7

1. breakfast
2. milk
3. egg
4. bread
5. lunch
6. meatball

7 pasta
8 dinner
9 rice
10 beans
11 fish
12 potatoes
13 chicken
14 peas

23.8

1 Fish and beans.
2 Milk and bread.
3 Meat and potatoes.
4 Chicken and peas.
5 Meatballs and rice.

23.9

1 Fish and potatoes.
2 What's for dinner?
3 Pasta and meatballs.

24

24.1

1 boy
2 girl
3 baby
4 woman
5 women
6 person
7 people
8 child/kid
9 children/kids
10 man
11 men

24.2

1 A
2 A
3 B

24.3

1 children
2 men
3 girl
4 woman
5 boy

24.4

1 man
2 kids
3 baby
4 boy

24.5

1 A
2 B
3 A
4 A
5 B

24.6

1 Is this Kim's ball?
2 Is this Nick's cat?
3 Is this Amy's book?
4 Is this Lucy's computer?
5 Is this Maria's jacket?

24.7

1 Ann
2 Matt
3 Kim
4 Sam
5 Andy

24.8

1 

2 

3 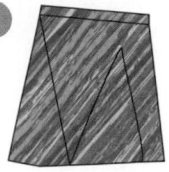

4 

5 

24.9

1 It's his. 2 It's ours. 3 It's yours.
4 It's theirs.

24.10

1 It's **his**.
2 It's **ours**.
3 It's **mine**.
4 It's **yours**.
5 It's **theirs**.
6 It's **hers**.
7 It's **ours**.

25

25.1

1 I get up.
2 I make my bed.
3 I eat breakfast.
4 I brush my teeth.
5 I walk to school.
6 I study English.
7 I eat lunch.
8 I go home.
9 I call my friend.
10 I go swimming.
11 I eat dinner.
12 I go to sleep.

25.2

1 I go home.
2 I get up.
3 I eat dinner.
4 I go swimming.
5 I study English.

25.3

1 I call my friend.
2 I walk to school.
3 I go to sleep.
4 I brush my teeth.
5 I eat lunch.

25.4

1 It's ten o'clock.
2 It's five o'clock.
3 It's one o'clock.
4 It's six o'clock.
5 It's four o'clock.
6 It's nine o'clock.
7 It's three o'clock.
8 It's eleven o'clock.

25.5

1. In the afternoon
2. In the evening
3. At night

25.6

1. I walk to school in the **morning**.
2. I eat dinner in the **evening**.
3. I go home in the **afternoon**.
4. I go to sleep at **night**.
5. I make my bed in the **morning**.

25.7

1. **When do you** get up?
2. I eat dinner **in** the evening.
3. I go to sleep **at** eight o'clock.
4. I go home at **four o'clock**.
5. I brush my teeth in the **morning** and at night.

25.8

1. We walk to school.
2. She calls her friend.
3. He brushes his teeth.
4. They eat dinner.
5. I go home.

25.9

1. Tuesday
2. Wednesday
3. Thursday
4. Friday
5. Saturday
6. Sunday

25.10

1. I go swimming **on** Tuesdays.
2. I call my friend **on** Fridays.
3. I eat lunch **at** twelve o'clock.

25.11

1. I don't.
2. I don't.
3. So do I.

Acknowledgments

The publisher would like to thank:

Ankita Awasthi Tröger for administrative assistance; Elizabeth Blakemore for editorial assistance; Laura Gardner for design assistance; Christine Stroyan, Kayla Dugger, Lori Hand, and Laura Caddell for proofreading; Christine Stroyan for audio script management and recording; and ID Audio for audio recording and production.

All images © Dorling Kindersley. For further information, visit **www.dkimages.com.**